Lessons From Carols

An Advent Devotional

Timothy J. Mulder

Editing assistance by Michelle Mulder, MD, Hannah Feuchtenberger
Musical assistance by Jeannie McCrocklin

ISBN: 979-8-9989882-3-3 (p)
ISBN: 979-8-9989882-4-0 (e)

Library of Congress Control Number: Applied for

Revision date: 10/07/2025

For the Christian Education classes at Southside Community Church.
You have blessed me far more than I ever blessed you.

Table of Contents

I

Introduction

The Son of God became a man to enable men to become sons of God.

C.S. Lewis

DURING THE HOLIDAY SEASON, CHRISTMAS carols are everywhere. They play on the radio, in the grocery store, and online. They are sung in churches, schools, community centers, and neighborhoods. They are an integral part of many Christmas celebrations. Going caroling is a tradition that has been around for 800 years. Christian or not, many of us grew up singing Christmas carols.

It makes sense, then, that we should study these carols. What are the stories behind them? What can we learn from those stories? What scriptural truths do they hold? Do they conflict with the Bible? These are questions that we will examine in each chapter.

Why Study Christmas Carols?
Christmas and Easter are the only two holy days that are also major secular holidays. The result is two different celebrations, each observed by millions of people. However, there is an awkward overlap between the two. Christians feel that the holiday is becoming more and more secular. This is why there is the movement among Christians to "Keep Christ in Christmas." However, those who celebrate "secular" Christmas can't help but find that the older meaning of Christmas keeps intruding uninvited upon their holiday. This is frequently experienced in traditional Christmas carols. Indeed, many traditional Christmas carols popularized in the 1930's by the likes of Bing Crosby, Nat King Cole, and others, have had modern renditions with key words changed to further distance them from a Christian message. For instance, Perry Como's "Walking in a Winter Wonderland" states that the couple would pretend a snowman was "Parson Brown." Modern versions has changed the identity of the snowman to a "circus clown."

Christmas caroling originally had nothing to do with Christmas or caroling. It was called "wassailing"[1] and consisted of groups of people visiting various homes to spread cheer during the winter months. There are some who maintain that wassailing began in pagan traditions. However, wassailing comes from two traditions: the singing to trees in the apple orchard to help bring about a good harvest, and the rowdy singing of songs at the homes of others. It wasn't until Francis of Assisi began to incorporate cheerful songs into Christmas services that caroling came about. He would teach the congregants Christmas songs and they would return home and share them with their neighbors. Christmas carols remain a great way to proclaim the love and peace of Christ to others. This is important, especially in a season riddled with anxiety and depression.

Is It scriptural?
When I was a worship pastor, one of the criteria I used when selecting music was that it had to be grounded in Scripture. I felt very strongly that if a song

---

[1] Wassail is the modern English spelling of the old English phrase *waes hael*, which means "good health!"

was not based on the Bible that we would not sing it in a worship service. This eliminated quite a bit of music. As you study the carols in this book, I challenge you to look at each of these carols in light of Scripture. While Christmas carols can be wonderful tools for devotion and evangelism, we must be cautious of them, as they are inspired by men and not God. As such, there can (and will) be discrepancies between carols and Scripture.

One question that arises regarding the biblical accuracy of Christmas carols is whether or not the angels sang at Jesus' birth. While the angels may very well have sung at His birth, there is no record of it in the four gospels. However, says Dr. Guy Waters, "Luke 2:13[2] uses a [Greek] verb (*ainéō*) that means to praise and, in what follows, the content of the praise resembles the sung praise of the Old Testament. If the "morning stars" (cf. "sons of God") of Job 38:7[3] are angels (as many take them to be), then we have record of the angels singing at creation. That corresponds to their singing at redemption. For that reason, I'm inclined to say that the angels did sing at the birth of Christ, though it is not made as explicit as it might have been."[4]

Another famous deviation from Scripture is contained in "Away in a Manger." The line, "But little Lord Jesus, no crying He makes," is problematic because we know that Jesus was born fully human. Babies cry to communicate their needs, expand their lung volume, and strengthen the muscles in their throat. As such, there is no reason to believe that Jesus did not cry like a normal baby. Additionally, we know that as an adult, Jesus wept. He certainly did so at the tomb of His friend Lazarus.[5] Therefore, there are some churches who will not sing this song because of this deviation from the Bible. And yet, many other churches will continue to sing it as it is a great tool with which to teach the Christmas story to young children. This is the kind of discrepancy in an otherwise good carol that doesn't necessarily warrant rejecting the carol

---

[2] Luke 2:13-14, "And suddenly there was with the angel a multitude of the heavenly host praising God and saying, [14] 'Glory to God in the highest, and on earth peace among those with whom He is pleased!'"

[3] Job 38:4-7, "Where were you when I laid the foundation of the earth? Tell me, if you have understanding. [5] Who determined its measurements—surely you know! Or who stretched the line upon it? [6] On what were its bases sunk, or who laid its cornerstone, [7] *when the morning stars sang together* and all the sons of God shouted for joy?" (Italics added.)

[4] Dr. Guy Waters, Professor of New Testament Studies at Reformed Theological Seminary personal correspondence to Timothy Mulder, July 21, 2025.

[5] John 11:34-37, "And He said, "Where have you laid him?" They said to Him, "Lord, come and see." [35] *Jesus wept.* [36] So the Jews said, "See how He loved him!" [37] But some of them said, "Could not He who opened the eyes of the blind man also have kept this man from dying?" (Italics added.)

outright. Rather, you may consider this a teaching point as you sing this song with your children.

Why Bring Up Theology?

Theology is the study of God. However, as we discuss each carol, we will learn more about God. What we sing reflects what we know and believe about God. John Stott, in his commentary on Romans says, "Theology (our belief about God) and doxology (our worship of God) should never be separated. On the one hand, there can be no doxology without theology. It is not possible to worship an unknown God. On the other hand, there should be no theology without doxology. There is something fundamentally flawed about a purely academic interest in God. ... true knowledge of God will always lead us to worship.... Our place is on our faces before Him in adoration.[6]

> *No priest, no theologian stood at the manger of Bethlehem. And yet all Christian theology has its origin in the wonder of all wonders: that God became human. Holy theology arises from knees bent before the mystery of the divine child in the stable.*
>
> Dietrich Bonhoeffer, *God is in the Manger,* 28.

This study is designed for family or individual devotions. It contains 28 short lessons and their corresponding carols. It is designed so that each lesson can be completed during each day of Advent. (Please note that sometimes lyrics have been changed to reflect the original lyrics of the carol.)

---

[6] John Stott, *The Message of Romans.* (Downers Grove: IVP, 2001), 311-312.

The music in this book has been arranged by the author
and can be found online in pdf form at:

https://www.armchairtheology.org/carols

Scan me!

Angels from the Realms of Glory

1. An - gels, from the realms of glo - ry, wing your flight o'er all the earth;
2. Shep-herds, in the fields a - bid - ing, watch - ing o'er your flocks by night;
3. Sag - es, leave your con - tem-pla - tions, Bright - er vi - sions beam a - far;
4. Saints be - fore the al - tar bend - ing, Watch - ing long in hope and fear,
5. Sin - ners, wrung with true re-pent - ance, Doomed for guilt to end - less pains,

Ye who sang cre - a - tions sto - ry, now pro - claim Mes - si - ah's birth:
God with man is now re-sid - ing, Yon - der shines the in - fant Light:
Seek the great De - sire of na - tions, Ye have seen His na - tal star.
Sud - den - ly the Lord, de-scend - ing, In His tem - ple shall ap - pear.
Jus - tice now re - vokes your sen - tence, Mer - cy calls you; break your chains.

Come and wor - ship, come and wor - ship, Wor - ship Christ the new-born King.

James Montgomery, 1816
Arr. Timothy Mulder, 2025

1

Angels from the Realms of Glory

MATTHEW 2:11A

And going into the house, they saw the child with Mary His mother,
and they fell down and worshiped Him.

"ANGELS FROM THE REALMS OF Glory" was written by Scottish newspaper editor James Montgomery. Montgomery was a prolific hymnist, penning over 400 hymns in his lifetime. British hymnologist J.R. Watson says, "James Montgomery was a well-known poet, highly thought of by his contemporaries such as Shelley and Byron."

Montgomery's father was a minister. When he was six, his parents left England to serve as missionaries in the West Indies. Montgomery stayed behind in England and attended boarding school there. Early on, inspired by the hymns of the Moravians,[7] he began writing poetry. In his teen years, he worked for the newspaper, *The Sheffield Register*. In time, Montgomery became editor, changing the name of the paper to *The Sheffield Iris*. He remained the editor there for over thirty years.

James Montgomery's full-time job was as a newspaper editor, but he wrote hymns and poetry on the side. He used his position to publish his poetry and hymns to spread the gospel in Sheffield. On Christmas Eve in 1816, "Angels from the Realms of Glory" was first published. Montgomery's life shows us that we do not have to be in full-time ministry positions to share the gospel effectively. Therefore, we, too, in secular employment and, indeed, in all of life, must use our circumstances to praise God and share His Word with a world desperately in need of it.

Modern hymnals, for the most part, have replaced Montgomery's final stanza with something more "upbeat." The original stanza read:

> Sinners, wrung with true repentance,
> Doomed for guilt to endless pains,
> Justice now revokes your sentence,
> Mercy calls you; break your chains.

The hymnal publishers felt that ending a joyful Christmas carol with such lyrics would dampen the emotions elicited by the hymn. The theme of the carol is the worship of Christ and each of the five stanzas provides a different aspect of worship. Lyrically, there is an intentional progression from the angels' song (stanza 1) to the shepherd's adoration (stanza 2) to the magi's' gifts (stanza 3) to the saints praising Him in heaven (stanza 4) to repenting sinners (stanza 5). Luke 15:7 says, "Just so, I tell you, there will be more joy in heaven over one sinner who repents than over ninety-nine righteous persons who need no repentance." When we look at stanza 5 in light of Luke 15:7, we see that there can be no greater joy than over one sinner who repents. Therefore, Montgomery's final stanza should leave the singer on a high note.

"Angels From the Realms of Glory" contains lyrics about the angels singing at creation. This is found in the first verse, "Ye who sang creation's story." The creation account found in Genesis 1-2, does not mention angels singing. However, as mentioned in the Introduction, if the "morning stars" and

---

[7] The Moravians were a Protestant Christian denomination that originated in the 15th century in what is now the Czech Republic.

the "sons of God" from Job 38:7[8] are angels then we have record of the angels singing at creation. In regard to angels singing, renowned preacher Charles Spurgeon said, "They sang, 'Glory to God on high, and on earth peace, good will towards men.' I think they sang it with gladness in their eyes; with their hearts burning with love, and with breasts as full of joy as if the good news to man had been good news to themselves."[9]

The angels at the world's creation were the same ones proclaiming the birth of Emmanuel. The shepherds, carrying on with their daily jobs, had their lives interrupted by the Son of God. They would never be the same after worshiping Him. The wise men left their positions of authority in exchange for kneeling at the cradle of the Son of the Most High. In doing so, they acknowledged their position in the universe: servants of the one true God. The saints in heaven watched as the Son of God humbled Himself and became human, to the point of being a servant, shedding His innocent blood for the remission of the sins of a mankind that hated Him. Sinners, when faced with the reality of Emmanuel, have no choice but to repent at His very being. No matter what part of life we come from, we are to worship Christ, the newborn King.

---

[8] Job 38:4-7, "Where were you when I laid the foundation of the earth? Tell me, if you have understanding. [5] Who determined its measurements—surely you know! Or who stretched the line upon it? [6] On what were its bases sunk, or who laid its cornerstone, [7] *when the morning stars sang together* and all the sons of God shouted for joy?" (Italics added.)

[9] Charles Spurgeon, "The First Christmas Carol." Sermon Delivered on Sunday, December 20, 1857, at the Music Hall, Royal Surrey Gardens.

Angels We Have Heard on High

1. An - gels we have heard on high, sweet - ly sing - ing o'er the plains,
2. Shep-herds, why this ju - bi-lee? Why your joy - ous strains pro-long?
3. Come to Beth - le - hem, and see Him whose birth the an - gels sing;

And the moun - tains in re - ply, ech - o back their joy - ous strains.
Say what may the tid - ings be which in - spire your heav'n - ly song?
Come, a - dore on bend - ed knee Christ the Lord, the new - born King.

Glo_____ ri - ia in ex-cel-sis De - o! Glo____

_____ ri - a in ex - cel - sis De - o!

James Chadwick, 1862
Arr. Timothy Mulder, 2025

2

Angels We Have Heard on High

───────❦───────

LUKE 2:14

*Glory to God in the highest, and on earth peace
among those with whom He is pleased!*

IN 130 A.D., POPE TELESPHORUS decreed that on the day celebrating Jesus' birth, all churches were to have special evening services. At these services, after the reading of Scripture, the congregation was to sing "Gloria in excelsis deo." This practice was common in most churches by the third century.

"Angels We Have Heard on High" is loosely based on the French song, "Les Anges dans nos Campagnes," which means "the angels in our countryside." In 1862, Roman Catholic bishop James Chadwick added his lyrics to some of the translated carol and set it to the tune of the traditional French hymn "Gloria."

In this carol, God has combined three seemingly unrelated elements—a French carol, James Chadwick's lyrics, and an early church chorus—to create something designed to praise Him. Luke 19:40[10] tells us that if people are silent about praising God, the stones will cry out instead. Through this carol, God has been praised for thousands of years in many cultures. All things will ultimately be brought to praise Him.

"Angels We Have Heard on High" is a carol that invites others to celebrate the birth of Jesus. The carol begins with an exciting stanza lauding the angels' celebration of Christ's birth. The first stanza is sung by the shepherds high up in the mountains. While they are "on high," they hear the angels singing over the plains. The mountains then echo the angels' song. The chorus is repeated to sound as though it echoes back from the mountains.

> *A great Christian life, or a great sermon, or a great song have a way of showing Christ to be so vast and glorious that our response can only be to humble ourselves, to bow down on bended knee and to acknowledge and be in awe of the greatness of our God. I think this carol enables us to do that really well.*
>
> Keith Getty

The second stanza has the vocalist asking the shepherds why the angels are celebrating. It must have been mind-blowing for the shepherds to witness a sky filled with worshiping angels. The third stanza invites us to join in the celebration. We are to worship the newborn King on bended knee. Each stanza finishes with the chorus, "Gloria in excelsis Deo," which is Latin for "Glory to God in the highest," a direct quote from Luke 2:14.

The third stanza invites the listener to Bethlehem to see Christ, the newborn King. Like the first humans to hear the angels' proclamation of Christ's birth, we can raise our voices in joyous song and join our praises with all the church since the second century.

---

[10] Luke 19:40, "He answered, "I tell you, if these were silent, the very stones would cry out.""

Jesus commands us in Matthew 28:19-20 to "make disciples of all nations, baptizing them in the name of the Father and of the Son and of the Holy Spirit, teaching them to observe all that I have commanded you." There are many ways to share the gospel with others. We do not have to go door to door to tell people about Jesus. (Although that is a great way to do so!) Another way to share the gospel is by singing carols and celebrating Christmas. We can fellowship with Christians and non-Christians together. We can invite friends to outreach events, Christian concerts, or Bible studies. Many non-Christians will attend candle-light services to celebrate Christmas with their families. Christmas is one of the best times to invite others to church. How will you share the good news of Jesus Christ with others this holiday season?

As With Gladness Men of Old

1.As   with   glad - ness   men   of   old   Did   the   guid - ing   star   be - hold;
2.As   with   joy - ful   steps   they   sped   To   that   low - ly   man - ger   bed,
3.As   they   of - fered   gifts   most   rare   At   that   man - ger   rude   and   bare,
4.Ho - ly   Je - sus,   ev - 'ry   day   Keep   us   in   the   nar - row   way;
5.In   the   heav'n - ly   count - ry   bright   need   they   no   cre - at - ed   light;

As   with   joy   they   hailed   its   light,   Lead - ing   on - ward,   beam-ing   bright;
There   to   bend   the   knee   be - fore   Him   whom   heav'n   and   earth   a - dore;
So   may   we   with   ho - ly   joy,   pure   and   free   from   sin's   al - loy,
And   when   earth - ly   things   are   past,   Bring   our   ran - somed   souls   at   last
Thou   its   light,   its   joy,   its   crown,   Thou   its   sun   which   goes   not   down;

So,   most   gra - cious   Lord,   may   we   ev - er - more   be   led   to   Thee.
So   may   we   with   will - ing   feet   ev - er   seek   Thy   mer - cy   seat.
All   our   cost - liest   trea - sures bring,   Christ,   to   Thee,   our   heav'n - ly   King.
Where   they   need   no   star   to   guide,   Where   no   clouds   Thy   glo - ry   hide.
There   for - ev - er   may   we   sing   al - le - lu - ias   to   our   King.

William Chatterton Dix, 1860
Arr. Timothy Mulder, 2025

3

As With Gladness Men of Old

MATTHEW 2:10

When they saw the star, they rejoiced exceedingly with great joy.

"AS WITH GLADNESS MEN OF Old" tells the story of the Magi's visitation of the Christ child, as found in Matthew 2:1-12. It was written by Scottish marine insurance agent William Chatterton Dix, who wrote poetry in his spare time. He wrote "As With Gladness Men of Old" while bed-ridden for months with severe depression. He wrote the carol on January 6, 1859, the Sunday of Epiphany,[11] when the visit of the Magi is traditionally celebrated. Legend says

---

[11] Epiphany is the day when the church celebrates the revelation of Jesus to the Gentiles.

that Dix wrote all the lyrics in a single day. The hymn was included in *Hymns for Public Worship and Private Devotion*.

The music for the carol was written by hymnal editor William Henry Monk. He based the song on a melody written by Stuttgart (Germany) organist Conrad Kocher. Personally, Dix did not care for the tune, but it quickly became popular and remains the version we sing today. The same melody is used in the hymn, "For the Beauty of the Earth." Eventually, Dix published the carol in his self-published hymnal, *Hymns of Joy and Love*.

Five years later, William Chatterton Dix would write another famous Christmas carol, "What Child is This?"

The first stanza of this carol speaks of the Magi being led by the star to see Jesus and includes a prayer in which the vocalist asks God that they, too, may be led to Him. The second stanza speaks of the Magi worshiping Jesus on bended knee and asking God for the willingness to approach Him. The third stanza speaks of the offerings of the Magi and invites the listener to bring their treasures to Jesus. The fourth stanza is a plea for salvation, and the fifth stanza describes heaven.

The carol combines the story of the Magi's visit with a personal prayer that we, too, might seek Jesus and receive salvation from Him. In addition to "As With Gladness, Men of Old," there is only one other popular Christmas carol on the topic of the Magi: "We Three Kings of Orient Are." It is important that we sing about this aspect of the Nativity story, as it speaks of Jesus' first interactions with Gentiles.[12] As Christians, we do not believe that Jesus came to save only the Jews, but that He came to offer salvation to everyone. Jesus has called believers from every culture, race, and time. He did not limit the scope of salvation to the Jews. In fact, during His time on earth, Jesus ministered to a Roman centurion,[13] the Samaritan woman at the well,[14] those in the Decapolis,[15] and the Syrophoenician woman,[16] among others.

In the fifth stanza's description of heaven,[17] the focus is on God as the source of light. This stanza is thoroughly scriptural, as it summarizes Revelation 21:22-25,

---

[12] A Gentile is someone who is not a Hebrew or a Jew.
[13] Matthew 8:5-13 and Luke 7:1-10.
[14] John 4:7-42.
[15] Mark 5:18-20 and Mark 7:31-37.
[16] Matthew 15:21-28 and Mark 7:24-30.
[17] Heaven is also referred to as the New Jerusalem or the City of God.

And I saw no temple in the city, for its temple is the Lord God the Almighty and the Lamb. And the city has no need of sun or moon to shine on it, for the glory of God gives it light, and its lamp is the Lamb. By its light will the nations walk, and the kings of the earth will bring their glory into it, and its gates will never be shut by day— and there will be no night there.

The temple was a human dwelling set aside as holy and provided a place for man to meet with God. In heaven, there is no need for a temple because the Lord God Almighty is the temple. According to these verses, Jesus is the lamp that lights the world.[18] By Him, the nations will walk in the light and all rulers of the earth will give Him glory. Indeed, there will be no night in the heavenly city, since Jesus Christ will provide all the light.

The final line of the carol's fifth verse, "There forever may we sing, Alleluias to our King" also describes heaven. Revelation 19:1 says, "After this I heard what seemed to be the loud voice of a great multitude in heaven, crying out, "Hallelujah! Salvation and glory and power belong to our God!"

The carol paints a wonderful picture of the listener joining the wise men on their journey to visit Jesus. This very same Jesus, who, after His resurrection, now serves as the lamp of the glory of God in heaven. O that we should all seek this wonderful Savior!

---

[18] John 8:12, "Again Jesus spoke to them, saying, "I am the light of the world. Whoever follows me will not walk in darkness, but will have the light of life."

Away in A Manger

1. A - way in a man - ger, no crib for a bed, The
2. The cat - tle are low - ing, the Ba - by a - wakes, But
3. Be near me, Lord Je - sus, I ask Thee to stay close

lit - tle Lord Je - sus laid down His sweet head; the
lit - tle Lord Je - sus, no cry - ing He makes; I
by me for - ev - er, and love me, I pray; Bless

stars in the sk - y looked down where He lay, The
love Thee, Lord Je - sus, look down from the sky And
all the dear child - ren in Thy ten - der care, And

lit - tle Lord Je - sus, a - sleep on the hay.
stay by my cra - dle til morn - ing is nigh.
fit us for heav - en, to live with Thee there.

Lyrics: James Murray, 1885
Music: William J. Kirkpatrick, 1895
Arr. Timothy Mulder, 2025

4

Away in a Manger

———————◈———————

LUKE 2:7

*And she gave birth to her firstborn son and wrapped Him in
swaddling cloths and laid Him in a manger,
because there was no place for them in the inn.*

THE STORY BEHIND "AWAY IN a Manger" is steeped in legend. Purportedly, Martin Luther wrote the carol, calling it "Luther's Cradle Hymn," which he sang to his children each night before bed. The story became even more exaggerated, claiming that thousands of German mothers sang it to their children while rocking them to sleep. During World Wars I and II, the tune was changed to the Scottish tune, "Flow Gently Sweet Afton," as a protest against all things German. However, after each war, the carol reverted to its "Lutheran" melody. It is humorous that not only was the song not German, but it was also not written by Luther.

The lyrics were first published in *Christmas Carols, New and Old,* in 1885. It was attributed to American composer James Ramsey Murray. The melody was written by American Composer William J. Kirkpatrick in 1895. Kirkpatrick's version has been sung in the United States for over one hundred years. The carol is one hundred percent "made in America."

"Away in a Manger" is frequently one of the first Christmas songs parents teach their children. The simple words and melody make it easy for most young ones to remember and understand. The beauty of the lullaby/carol is the poignant reminder of Jesus' humble beginnings. According to Ace Collins, "The serene picture painted in the carol's lyrics defines 'peace on Earth' better than most books or sermons."[19]

Like many Christmas carols, the carol begins by describing one aspect of the Christmas story and then shifts to a personal prayer in which the vocalist asks God to draw them closer to Him. In that aspect, "Away in a Manger" is another carol that invites the listener into a relationship with Jesus. The third stanza has a marked shift from the first two, taking the focus from the baby Jesus in His manger to the salvation of all children in His care. John 10:28-30[20] speaks of those in His care, "I give them eternal life, and they will never perish, and no one will snatch them out of my hand." Jesus – the very one born in the humble circumstances of a stable – is so powerful, that He will protect all those entrusted to Him. He will not allow anyone to snatch them out of His hand. Once we belong to Him, we will always belong to Him. Romans 8:38-39 emphasize this, "For I am sure that neither death nor life, nor angels nor rulers, nor things present nor things to come, nor powers, nor height nor depth, nor anything else in all creation, will be able to separate us from the love of God in Christ Jesus our Lord." Nothing can separate us from God's love. And that is perhaps the most important truth in this life.

As discussed in the Introduction, one line in the second stanza is not biblical. The line reads, "but little Lord Jesus, no crying He makes." There is

---

[19] Ace Collins, *Stories Behind the Best-Loved Songs of Christmas.* (Grand Rapids: Zondervan, 2001), 24.
[20] John 10:28-30, "I give them eternal life, and they will never perish, and no one will snatch them out of my hand. [29] My Father, who has given them to me, is greater than all, and no one is able to snatch them out of the Father's hand. [30] I and the Father are one."

no evidence that Jesus never cried as a baby. Hebrews 2:17[21] tells us that Jesus was "made like His brothers in every respect," including displaying human emotions. We do know that Jesus wept at the tomb of Lazarus before he was raised from the dead.[22]

"Away in A Manger" is a beautiful carol that focuses on the humble circumstances in which Jesus came to earth. Being born in a stable and bedded in a feed trough is the obvious aspect of the unassuming circumstances of His birth. But it is even more profound that Jesus left the throne of Heaven to take on the flesh of a helpless human baby.

Philippians 2:6-8 speaks of Christ's humility in coming to earth, "who, though He was in the form of God, did not count equality with God a thing to be grasped, but emptied Himself, by taking the form of a servant, being born in the likeness of men. And being found in human form, He humbled Himself by becoming obedient to the point of death, even death on a cross." Jesus not only had humble beginnings in His life on earth, but He remained humble through His death on the cross. However, as Philippians 2:9-11 continues, we read that "God has highly exalted Him and bestowed on Him the name that is above every name, so that at the name of Jesus every knee should bow, in heaven and on earth and under the earth, and every tongue confess that Jesus Christ is Lord, to the glory of God the Father." Despite Jesus' lowly beginnings, God has exalted Him and given Him the name that is above all names. Everyone will ultimately bow before Him and confess that He is Christ the Lord. What a glorious day that shall be!

---

[21] Hebrews 2:17, "Therefore He had to be made like His brothers in every respect, so that He might become a merciful and faithful High Priest in the service of God, to make propitiation for the sins of the people."

[22] John 11:35, "Jesus wept."

Come Thou Long Expected Jesus

1. Come, Thou long expected Jesus, Born to set Thy people free;
2. Joy to those who long to see Thee, Day-spring from on high appear;
3. Come to earth to taste our sadness, He whose glories knew no end;
4. Born Thy people to deliver, born a Child and yet a King.

From our fears and sins release us; Let us find our rest in Thee.
Come Thou promised Rod of Jesse, of Thy birth we long to hear!
by His life He brings us gladness, our Redeemer, Shepherd, Friend.
Born to reign in us forever, now Thy gracious kingdom bring.

Israel's strength and consolation, Hope of all the earth Thou art;
O'er the hills the angels singing news, glad tidings of a birth:
Leaving riches without number, born within a cattle stall;
By Thine own eternal Spirit, rule in all our hearts alone;

Dear desire of ev'ry nation, Joy of ev'ry longing heart.
"Go to Him, your praises bringing; Christ the Lord has come to earth."
this the everlasting wonder, Christ was born the Lord of all.
by Thine all-sufficient merit, raise us to Thy glorious throne.

Stanzas 1,4, Charles Wesley, 1744
Stanzas 2-3, Mark E. Hunt, 1978.
Arr. Timothy Mulder, 2025

5

Come Thou Long Expected Jesus

LUKE 2:25

Now there was a man in Jerusalem, whose name was Simeon,
and this man was righteous and devout,
waiting for the consolation of Israel, and the Holy Spirit was upon him.

ONE OF THE PRIMARY THEMES of Advent is anticipation. Jesus' parents eagerly anticipated His birth. The shepherds anticipated going to see the child of whom the angels spoke. The Magi anticipated witnessing the child they had traveled so long to see. During the holiday season, children eagerly anticipate opening gifts on Christmas morning and adults anticipate feasting and celebrating with friends and family. The Christmas carol "Come Thou Long-Expected Jesus" perfectly captures this feeling of anticipation. It echoes the hopes and cries of every heart.

The lyrics to the first and fourth stanzas were written in 1744 by Charles Wesley. Despite their short length, Wesley's two stanzas are rich in meaning, relying heavily on Old Testament prophecy and employing the language of the King James Bible. In 1978, Mark E. Hunt added the second and third stanzas. Hunt also used the King James Bible for his two stanzas, seamlessly adding to Wesley's original stanzas.

Initially, the carol was put to the melody of "Stuttgart," written in 1716 by German composer Christian Friedrich Witt. However, in the mid-1800's, the melody was changed to "Hyfrydol," which means "beautiful" in Welsh. The melody was written by Rowland Hugh Prichard in 1855 for inclusion in a children's songbook. The melody is very popular with hymnists, as it is used for the hymns "What a Friend We Have in Jesus," "Love Divine All Loves Excelling," "Alleluia! What a Savior," as well as "Come Thou Long Expected Jesus."

The popularity of the carol skyrocketed after Charles Spurgeon used it in a Christmas sermon in 1855. Spurgeon spoke of how Jesus was the only one to be born a king without first being a prince. After Spurgeon's sermon, the hymn became widespread, gaining inclusion in hymnals of various denominations.

The viewpoint of the hymn is grounded in the hope of the Old Testament Jews for the coming Messiah. The lyrics present Jesus as the fulfillment of that hope. Wesley and Hunt looked beyond Christ's first coming to His second. The anticipation of the nativity as communicated in the carol foreshadows the longing for Christ's return. The biblically sound lyrics present the anticipation of the coming Messiah through descriptions of Him. The lyrics tell what Christ will do: set His people free, release us from our fears and sins, deliver us, rule in our hearts, and raise us to His glorious throne. They also describe who He is: Israel's strength and consolation, the hope of all of the earth, the desire of every nation, and the joy of every longing heart.

Luke 2:22-38 tells the stories of Simeon and Anna. Simeon was an older man who lived in Jerusalem and had been eagerly awaiting the coming Messiah. God promised Simeon that he would not die until he had seen Him. On the eighth day after Jesus' birth, Mary and Joseph brought Jesus to the temple to be circumcised and presented to God. When Simeon saw Jesus, he picked Him up in his arms and blessed Him, saying, "Lord, now you are letting your servant depart in peace, according to your word; for my eyes have seen your salvation that you have prepared in the presence of all peoples, a light for revelation to the Gentiles, and for glory to your people Israel."[23]

Anna was an elderly prophetess who lived in the temple, fasting, worshiping, and praying. She was also in the temple when Mary and Joseph entered with Jesus. Upon seeing the Christ child, Anna began giving thanks to God about Him to all who were waiting for the redemption of Jerusalem.

> *From eight days old, it was clear that Jesus came to save both Gentiles and Jews. Salvation would no longer be based on nationality.*

Both Simeon and Anna were blessed to be part of the fulfillment of the prophecy in Isaiah 9:6, "For to us a child is born, to us a son is given; and the government shall be upon His shoulder, and His name shall be called Wonderful Counselor, Mighty God, Everlasting Father, Prince of Peace." We can learn a lot from their responses to witnessing Emmanuel. Simeon began praising God for fulfilling His promise and for sending a light for Gentiles and Jews. Anna not only gave thanks for the arrival of Jesus, but she began telling those around her about the one who would redeem Jerusalem and all of His chosen people. Our response in coming to know Jesus should mirror Simeon and Anna; we are to praise and thank God for sending salvation. We are also to tell those with whom we come into contact to eagerly anticipate His return.

---

[23] Luke 2:29-32

Gentle Mary Laid Her Child

1.Gen - tle Ma - ry laid her Child low - ly in a man - ger;
2.An - gels sang a - bout His birth; wise men sought and found Him;
3.Gen - tle Ma - ry laid her Child low - ly in a man - ger;

There He lay, the Un - de - filed, To the world a stran - ger:
Heav - en's star shone bright - ly forth, Glo - ry all a - round Him:
He is still the Un - de - filed, but no more a stran - ger.

Such a Babe in such a place, Can He be the Sav - ior?
Shep - herds saw the won - drous sight, Heard the an - gels sing - ing;
Son of God of hum - ble birth, beau - ti - ful the sto - ry;

Ask the saved of all the race, Who have found His fa - vor?
All the plains were lit that night, All the hills were ring - ing.
Praise His name in all the earth, Hail the King of glo - ry!

Joseph Simpson Cook, 1919
Arr. Timothy Mulder, 2025

6

Gentle Mary Laid Her Child

———— ❧ ————

LUKE 2:7

And she gave birth to her firstborn son and wrapped Him in swaddling cloths
And laid Him in a manger, because there was no place for them in the inn.

"GENTLE MARY LAID HER CHILD" has perhaps the most interesting backstory of all the carols. In October 1919, the Canadian newspaper, *The Christian Guardian*, held a Christmas carol contest. The contest was broken into two parts: lyrics and music. Submission for lyrics ended on October 28, and prizes for the lyrics were $20 for first place, $10 for second, and $5 for third place. Joseph Simpson Cook, a Canadian Methodist preacher, submitted his winning poem originally titled, "Gentle Mary Wrapped Her Child." After Cook's win, the second portion of the contest began. The paper received multiple submissions for accompaniment to Cook's lyrics, with prizes going out to the three winners. However, none of those melodies are the one we sing today.

The melody used today is *Tempus Adest Floridum*, a popular Scandinavian tune from the fourteenth century. It is the same one used in the Christmas carol, "Good King Wenceslas." It was harmonized by Ernest C. MacMillan, a Canadian organist, conductor, and composer. The music has a cheery, robust melody, which does not quite fit with the introspective words found in each stanza. Over the years, hymnal editors and composers have attempted to put the lyrics to a newer melody. However, because the final line of the fourth stanza, "Praise His name in all the earth! Hail the King of Glory!" fits with the music, the melody has continued to be used over the years. Somewhere along the way, when MacMillan placed the poem in his arrangement, the lyrics of the first stanza and the title were changed from "Gentle Mary wrapped her Child" to "Gentle Mary laid her Child." The shift from "wrapped" to "laid" fits the subdued feel of the lyrics better.

> *The advent story is the most wonderful rescue story ever.*
> *The Son of God left His Father's side and became a man*
> *to rescue us from us.*
>
> Paul David Tripp

Lyrically, "Gentle Mary Laid Her Child" explores the significance of the Christ-child. It begins with the humble circumstances surrounding His birth and then asks if He could be the Savior. The lyrics then direct the singer to ask those who have been saved. Stanza 2 speaks of those who visited Jesus in His lowly surroundings: the angels, the wise men, and the shepherds. Everything in the second stanza points to the glory of Jesus Christ. This should be true in our lives as well. Everything we do should point to Christ's glory. Stanza 3 describes Jesus as "still the undefiled," referencing his sinless life, and culminates in praising Jesus as the Son of God and King of Glory.

The text of the carol is soundly scriptural. The opening lines of the first and third stanzas are based on Luke 2:7, "And she gave birth to her firstborn Son and wrapped Him in swaddling cloths and laid Him in a manger, because there was no place for them in the inn." Hebrews 7:26 (KJV)[24] describes Jesus as our "undefiled" High Priest. John 1:10 speaks of Jesus being a stranger to all the world, "He was in the world, and the world was made through Him, yet the world did not know Him." Despite creating the world, Jesus was initially a stranger to His creation. However, His life on earth made Him "no longer a stranger," as the second stanza states. The second stanza summarizes the appearance of the angels to the shepherds as found in Luke 2:8-14[25] as well as the arrival of the wise men as found in Matthew 2:1-2,[26] 9-11.[27]

"Gentle Mary Laid Her Child" serves as an excellent summary of the Christmas story, emphasizing Christ's lowly beginnings, sinless life, and His position of glory after His resurrection. Its beautiful lyrics emphasize His sinless life and His incarnation as a man, both part of God's glorious plan to make Him the propitiation for our sins. It may not be as popular as other Christmas carols, but it is a wonderful hymn of praise.

---

[24] Hebrews 7:26 (KJV), "For such a High Priest became us, who is holy, harmless, undefiled, separate from sinners, and made higher than the heavens."

[25] Luke 2:8-14, "And in the same region there were shepherds out in the field, keeping watch over their flock by night. [9] And an angel of the Lord appeared to them, and the glory of the Lord shone around them, and they were filled with great fear. [10] And the angel said to them, 'Fear not, for behold, I bring you good news of great joy that will be for all the people. [11] For unto you is born this day in the city of David a Savior, who is Christ the Lord. [12] And this will be a sign for you: you will find a baby wrapped in swaddling cloths and lying in a manger.' [13] And suddenly there was with the angel a multitude of the heavenly host praising God and saying, [14] 'Glory to God in the highest, and on earth peace among those with whom He is pleased!'"

[26] Matthew 2:1-2, "Now after Jesus was born in Bethlehem of Judea in the days of Herod the king, behold, wise men from the east came to Jerusalem, [2] saying, 'Where is He who has been born king of the Jews? For we saw His star when it rose and have come to worship Him.'"

[27] Matthew 2:9-11, "After listening to the king, they went on their way. And behold, the star that they had seen when it rose went before them until it came to rest over the place where the child was. [10] When they saw the star, they rejoiced exceedingly with great joy. [11] And going into the house, they saw the child with Mary his mother, and they fell down and worshiped Him. Then, opening their treasures, they offered Him gifts, gold and frankincense and myrrh."

Go Tell It on the Mountain

Go tell it on the moun - tain o - ver the hills and ev - ery-where

Go tell it on the moun - tain that Je - sus Christ is born While
The
Down

shep – herds kept their watch – ing o'er si – lent flocks by night, be –
shep – herds feared and trem – bled when, lo! a – bove the earth rang
in a low – ly man – ger our hum – ble Christ was born, and

hold, through – out the heav – ens there shone a ho – ly light.
out the an – gel cho – rus that hailed our Sav – ior's birth.
God sent us sal – va – tion that bles – sed Christ – mas morn.

Lyrics: John Work II
Music: American Traditional
Arr. Timothy Mulder, 2025

7

Go Tell It on the Mountain

LUKE 2:17

*And when they saw it, they made known the saying
that had been told them concerning this child.*

THE HISTORY BEHIND "GO TELL It on the Mountain" is uncertain. The carol
was first included in a collection entitled *Religious Folk Songs of the Negro* in
1909. In that collection, it was subtitled "A Christmas Plantation Song."
Today's lyrics are attributed to Professor John Work II of Fisk University, who
penned them since the original stanzas could not be found. However, since his
publication, the original stanzas have been found, and while the chorus remains
the same, the stanzas read,

1. When I was a seeker, I sought both night and day,
    I ask de' Lord to help me, and He show me de way.
2. He chose me for His watchman, up on a city wall,
    If I am a Christian, I am de least of all.
3. In de town of David, some call Him a King,
    If ever a chile was true redeem', Christ Jesus'll hear him sing.

Today, we still sing Professor Work's stanzas using the original chorus. The melody of the song remains the same. Lyrically, we will look at Professor Work's stanzas since they pertain more to Christmas.

This carol tells the Christmas story from the shepherds' perspective. Stanza 1 begins with the shepherds watching "over their flocks by night."[28] In the time of Jesus, it was very common for shepherds to sleep near their sheep. Many of the shepherds were Bedouins who did not live in tents or houses but lived out in the open fields with their flocks year-round.[29] Skeptics of the Bible also question whether or not the shepherds would have had their sheep up in the Judean Mountains around Bethlehem during the winter. However, ranchers in California keep their sheep outdoors year-round. Since Bethlehem's climate is similar to California's, we can reasonably assume that the Judean shepherds also kept their sheep outdoors during the winter months.

The first stanza ends with a reference to a "holy light." Luke 2 describes the angel of the Lord being surrounded by the shining glory of the Lord.[30] The image described by the verse implies the darkness of the night sky suddenly lit up by a holy light. If you have ever camped in a remote area, you can understand the shepherds' awe because moonless or cloudy nights are pitch black without the noise of the lights of civilization. The dark fields exploding with light must have been awesome indeed. The second stanza continues with the shepherds being filled with "great fear," and continues to describe the angel chorus as they "hailed our Savior's birth." This is a minor departure from Scripture, in that Luke 2:14 describes the angels proclaiming, "Glory to God in the highest and on earth peace among those with whom He is pleased." However, the stanza summarizes the feeling of the angels' proclamation.

---

[28] Luke 2:8, "And in the same region there were shepherds out in the field, keeping watch *over their flock by night*." (Italics added.)

[29] https://www.fao.org/4/p8550e/P8550E01.htm Accessed March 28, 2025.

[30] Luke 2:9, "And an angel of the Lord appeared to them, and the glory of the Lord shone around them, and they were filled with great fear."

After the shepherds' fears were calmed, they followed the angel's instruction and went to Bethlehem to see the newborn Jesus. According to Luke 2:17-18,[31] on their way down from the Judean mountains, the shepherds told others about what they had seen and where they were going. Hence, the title, "Go Tell It on the Mountain."

The third stanza describes the scene when the shepherds arrived down in Bethlehem. Luke 2:16[32] tells us that they saw, "Mary and Joseph, and the baby lying in a manger." Luke 2:20[33] tells us that after the shepherds had witnessed Jesus in the manger, that they returned up into the mountains. Along the way, the shepherds were "glorifying and praising God for all they had heard and seen, as it had been told them."

After being frightened by the angels, traveling to Bethlehem, and witnessing the Son of God lying in a manger, the shepherds were changed people. Every person who came into contact with Jesus during His time on earth came away a changed person. This is what happens to us as well, when we have a relationship with Him—everything changes. We want to tell others about the joy that we have found in Him. This is what happened to the shepherds when they met Him. Overflowing with joy, they told everyone on the mountain, over the hills, and everywhere! And we are to do the same.

---

[31] Luke 2:18, "And when they saw it, they made known the saying that had been told them concerning this child. [18] And all who heard it wondered at what the shepherds told them."

[32] Luke 2:16, "And they went with haste and found Mary and Joseph, and the baby lying in a manger."

[33] Luke 2:20, "And the shepherds returned, glorifying and praising God for all they had heard and seen, as it had been told them."

God Rest Ye Merry Gentlemen

God rest ye mer - ry gen - tle - men, let noth - ing you dis - may, Re -
From God our heav'n - ly Fa - ther, a bless - ed an - gel came; and
"Fear not, then," said the an - gel, "let no - thing you a - fright; This
The shep - herds at those ti - dings re - joic - ed much in mind; and

mem - ber Christ our Sav - vior was born on Christ - mas day. To
un - to cer - tain shep - herds brought tid - ings of the same: How
day is born a Sav - vior of a pure vir - gin bright, To
left their flocks a - feed - ing in tem - pest storm and wind: and

save us all from, Sa - tan's pow'r when we were gone a - stray; O
that in Beth - le - hem was born the Son of God by name.
free all those who trust in Him from Sa - tan's pow'r and might."
went to Beth - le - hem straight - way, the Son of God to find.

ti - dings of com - fort and joy, com - fort and joy, O

ti - dings of com - fort and joy.

Music: Samuel Wesley
Arr. Timothy Mulder, 2025

8

God Rest Ye Merry Gentlemen

LUKE 2:10-11

And the angel said to them, "Fear not, for behold, I bring you good news of great joy that will be for all the people. For unto you is born this day in the city of David a Savior, who is Christ the Lord."

"GOD REST YE MERRY GENTLEMEN" is one of the most profound hymns sung in the church today. The carol's message is one of boundless joy. The chorus reminds us that the birth of Jesus should bring comfort and joy. Joy that Emmanuel[34] haσ been born and comfort in that this newborn Savior will save us from the power of Satan.

---

[34] Emmanuel means "God with us." Jesus, in becoming man, is Emmanuel.

The earliest version of "God Rest Ye Merry Gentlemen" dates back to around 1650. The first line was slightly different than the one we have today, reading, "Sit you merry gentlemen." The carol was first published on a broadsheet[35] in 1760. It was published a few years later in the English periodical, the *Monthly Review*. In 1833, the carol was printed in the *Oxford Book of Carols*, although the music is not what is sung today. The music we sing today is a traditional English melody written by Samuel Wesley. The carol has been known as "The Old Christmas Carol" since the mid-1700s. "God Rest Ye Merry Gentlemen" is featured in Charles Dickens' *A Christmas Carol*. It is also quoted in George Eliot's novel *Silas Marner*.

When the carol was written, most church music had a dark, somber tone. Many of the congregants did not care for this style of music; instead, they preferred songs that had more joy and happiness, similar to rousing drinking songs. Many of today's Christmas carols came out of a desire to marry the infectious joy of popular ballads with scriptural lyrics, of which "God Rest Ye Merry Gentlemen" is the most famous. The song evoked feelings of happiness in those who sang and danced to it. Says Ace Collins, "Though it might have been rejected by church leaders, "God Rest Ye Merry Gentlemen" better presented the message of the first Christmas and the life of Jesus than did many of the songs used in the formal worship of the day."[36]

The carol's first stanza is a concise presentation of the gospel. As human beings, we are often dismayed at the condition of this sinful world. But when we are down, we must remember that Christ our Savior was born. For those who are saved, this marks the beginning of the salvation process: the Savior's birth. The next lines in stanza 1 tell us why He has been born, "to save us all from Satan's power when we were gone astray." We have all succumbed to the temptation of sin in our lives and have gone astray. However, according to Romans 5:8, "God shows His love for us in that while *we were still sinners*, Christ died for us." (Italics added.) Christ didn't die for us after we got it all together and began living holy lives. Christ died for us when we still rejected Him and followed our sinful desires.

The second stanza focuses more on the Christmas story itself. It speaks of God the Father sending angels to the shepherds proclaiming the birth of the Son of God, and the third stanza tells of the interaction between the angels and the

---

[35] A broadsheet is a single piece of paper (much like a handbill) with a ballad, rhyme, or poem printed on it.
[36] Collins, 54.

shepherds. The first thing the angels told the shepherds was not to fear. (Throughout the Bible, whenever an angel appeared to someone, the first thing the angel said to them was, "Do not fear.") The angel then proceeded to tell the shepherds that "unto you is born this day in the city of David a Savior, who is Christ the Lord."[37] The stanza then returns to the gospel theme: "to free all those who trust in Him from Satan's power and might."

The fourth stanza provides the shepherds' reaction.[38] The shepherds responded immediately upon receiving the news of the Son of God being born in Bethlehem. They did not wait or contemplate what they should do. They rejoiced and left their flocks to seek the Son of God. Stanza four says that they left their flocks in tempest, storm, and wind. There is no biblical evidence of a tempest, storm, or wind. This is likely poetic hyperbole by the author that the shepherds were at the fields at night during the winter, as winters in Judea are typically mild, the depiction is more fitting for winters in Great Britain and would have resonated with their audience.

The chorus repeats the intent of the gospel message. The story of Christ's birth should fill us with joy as it did the first century shepherds. And the gospel message should be of great comfort to the sinner. And that is what this carol tells us to do: offer one another "tidings of comfort and joy." We are to share the gospel with joy!

---

[37] Luke 2:11.

[38] Luke 2:15-17, "When the angels went away from them into heaven, the shepherds said to one another, 'Let us go over to Bethlehem and see this thing that has happened, which the Lord has made known to us.' [16] And they went with haste and found Mary and Joseph, and the baby lying in a manger. [17] And when they saw it, they made known the saying that had been told them concerning this child."

Good Christian Men Rejoice

1.Good Chris - tian men, re - joice   With heart and soul and voice!
2.Good Chris - tian men, re - joice   With heart and soul and voice!
3.Good Chris - tian men, re - joice   With heart and soul and voice!

Give ye heed to what we say: Je - sus Christ is born to - day!
Now ye hear of end - less bliss: Je - sus Christ was born for this!
Now ye need not fear the grave; Je - sus Christ was born to save!

Ox and ass be - fore Him bow, And He is in the man - ger now.
He has o - pened heav - en's door, And man is bles - sed ev - er - more.
Calls you one and calls you all, To gain His ev - er - last - ing hall.

Christ is born to - day!   Christ is born to - day!
Christ was born for this!   Christ was born for this!
Christ was born to save!   Christ was born to save!

Heinrich Suso, 1327
James Mason Neale, 1850
Arr. Timothy Mulder, 2025

9

Good Christian Men Rejoice

PSALM 16:9

Therefore, my heart is glad, and my whole being rejoices;
my flesh also dwells secure.

"GOOD CHRISTIAN MEN REJOICE!" WAS written by two men ostracized by the church for their beliefs. The author was Heinrich Suso, the son of German nobility. Instead of remaining in the ruling class, Suso became a Dominican monk. In 1326, he published his first work, *The Little Book of Truth*, in which he justified sharing the gospel with lay people[39] in a way that would bring hope,

---

[39] Lay people are those that are not clergy.

compassion, and understanding. Suso's justification for sharing the gospel with ordinary people was the angels bringing the good news to the shepherds at the time of Christ's birth.[40] Instead of being known as one who shared the love of Christ with common people, he was tried for heresy. A year later, he published another work, *The Little Book of Eternal Wisdom*, which he wrote in German so it could be read by everyone. Unable to control the radical priest, the Pope condemned him, and he was exiled to Switzerland where he suffered terrible slander and persecution. Suso never backed down from his desire to share the gospel with commoners.

One night in a dream, Suso saw armies of angels singing and dancing. They sang the German words and the melody of "Good Christian Men Rejoice!" At the time, church music was still in the form of Gregorian chant: solemn, scriptural, and always written in Latin. Suso's hymn violated all three of these unspoken rules: The melody was joyful, and the German lyrics did not directly quote Scripture. The church did not adopt his hymn, but the common people loved it, singing it in their homes, pubs, and on their way to worship. It would be over 150 years before the hymn was published.

James Mason Neale was a priest in the Church of England whose work includes the hymn, "All Glory, Laud and Honor." His other famous Christmas carol is "O Come O Come Emmanuel." Neale wanted to bring the joy of salvation to the common man. Sadly, his views were considered radical and Neale was also exiled from his homeland. He served as a missionary on the North African island of Madeira. There, he began an order of women to feed the poor, take care of orphans, and minister to prostitutes. This group served tens of thousands of people. Around 1850, Neale translated "Good Christian Men Rejoice!" into English, where it was published in a collection entitled *Carols for Christmastide*. By 1900, the carol was immensely popular in Europe and America.

This carol provides three reasons why Jesus Christ came to earth: stanza one tells us that He came to earth for His glory, stanza two tells us that He came to give believers access to God the Father, and stanza three tells us that He came to save those who are called.

Other theology contained in this carol includes the command found in Matthew 10:27 that tells us to "*love the Lord your God with all your heart and with all your soul and with all your mind.*" (Italics added.) The chorus of this

---

[40] Luke 2:10, "And the angel said to them, "Fear not, for behold, I bring you good news of great joy that will be for *all the people.*" (Italics added.)

carol is similar, with "mind" being changed to "voice," as it rhymes better. Therefore, when we sing this carol, we are to rejoice with all of our being! This is based on Psalm 16:9 – "Therefore my heart is glad, and my whole being rejoices; my flesh also dwells secure."

God's Word describes several kinds of calling, including a general call to everyone and an effectual call to His people. "Good Christian Men Rejoice" discusses both. The general call is the call that goes out to everyone, as all are called to turn away from sin and to turn to God for our salvation. Luke 14:23 tells us, "And the master said to the servant, 'Go out to the highways and hedges and compel people to come in, that my house may be filled.'" The effectual call is when the Holy Spirit improves upon the general call and makes it effective. Those who respond to Christ in faith receive this effectual, internal call. John 6:44 says, "No one can come to me unless the Father who sent me draws him. And I will raise him up on the last day." This is likely something we never think about when we sing this carol – the fact that it adheres to biblical theology.

While the melody of this carol is upbeat in nature, it contains solid theology. It provides us with the reason behind the incarnation and links the necessity of the Savior's birth to the gospel. All in all, this ancient hymn is biblically and theologically solid and should be sung frequently throughout the Christmas season.

Hark! The Herald Angels Sing

1. Hark! the her - ald an - gels sing, "Glo - ry to the new - born King;
2. Christ, by high - est heav'n a - dored; Christ, the ev - er - last - ing Lord!
3. Hail, the heav'n - born Prince of Peace! Hail, the Son of Right - ous - ness!

Peace on earth and mer - cy mi - ld, God and sin - ners re - con - ciled!"
Late in time be - hold Him co - me, Off - spring of the Vir - gin's womb;
Light and life to all He br - ings, Ris'n with heal - ing in His wings.

Joy - ful, all ye na - tions rise, Join the tri - umph of the skies;
Veiled in flesh the God - head see, Hail the'in - car - nate De - i - ty,
Mild He lays His glo - ry by, Born that man no more may die,

With th'an - gel - ic host pro - claim, "Christ is born in Beth - le - hem."
Pleased as man with men to dwell, Je - sus our Em - man - u - el.
Born to raise the sons of earth, Born to give them sec - ond birth.

Hark! the her - ald an - gels sing, "Glo - ry to the new - born King!"
Hark! the her - ald an - gels sing, "Glo - ry to the new - born King!"
Hark! the her - ald an - gels sing, "Glo - ry to the new - born King!"

Charles Wesley, 1739
Felix Mendelssohn-Bartholdy, 1840
Arr. Timothy Mulder, 2025

10

Hark! The Herald Angels Sing

———————◦∞◦———————

LUKE 2:13-14

And suddenly there was with the angel a multitude of the heavenly host
praising God and saying, "Glory to God in the highest
and on earth peace among those with whom He is pleased!"

THE STORY OF "HARK! THE Herald Angels Sing" plays out like a soap opera.
The lyrics were written by Charles Wesley, the author of hymns such as "Christ
the Lord is Risen Today," and "Love Divine, All Loves Excelling." Wesley
penned the phrase, "Hark! How all the welkin rings, glory to the King of kings!"
Welkin is a five-dollar word for heavenly proclamation. This is precisely what
the angels did – they proclaimed the birth of Christ. Wesley put the carol to his

music, which became quite popular among congregations within the Methodist church.

However, George Whitefield, bartender turned Calvinist preacher, took liberty with Wesley's carol and changed the lyrics without Wesley's consent. Whitefield changed the lyric to "Hark! The herald angels sing!" Wesley was extremely upset as Whitefield's new lyrics were not scriptural. According to Wesley, the angels did not sing - they spoke. Wesley never sang Whitefield's version and died at odds with Whitefield over this and other theological issues.

William Cummings, a tenor who sang under Felix Mendelssohn, without the approval of Wesley, Whitefield, or Mendelssohn, put Whitefield's lyrics to Mendelssohn's "Festgesang an die Künstler," (Celebration Song for the Artist) which Mendelssohn had written in homage to Johann Gutenberg, the inventor of the printing press. The arrangement of Whitefield's stolen and altered Wesleyan lyrics, set to Mendelssohn's music, is the Christmas carol that we know and love and sing today.

What does this carol teach us about Jesus Christ? He is the "everlasting Lord," who came down from the "highest heaven" to be the "offspring of the virgin's womb." Why did Jesus come to earth? To see "God and sinners reconciled." How did He accomplish this? He "lays His glory by" that we "no more may die." How can this life be ours? Through an inward, spiritual regeneration called "the second birth." With a brilliant economy, this carol provides an excellent summary of the gospel. Tim Keller says, "To understand Christmas is to understand the gospel."[41]

The theological concept of reconciliation between God and sinners is also prominent. Man's reconciliation with God through Christ is the major theme of 2 Corinthians 5:16-21:

> From now on, therefore, we regard no one according to the flesh. Even though we once regarded Christ according to the flesh, we regard Him thus no longer. Therefore, if anyone is in Christ, he is a new creation. The old has passed away; behold, the new has come. All this is from God, *who through Christ reconciled us to Himself* and gave us the ministry of reconciliation; that is, in Christ, God was reconciling the world to Himself, not counting their trespasses against them, and entrusting to us the message of reconciliation. Therefore,

---

[41] Timothy Keller, *Hidden Christmas* (New York: Viking, 2016), 4.

we are ambassadors for Christ, God making His appeal through us. We implore you on behalf of Christ, *be reconciled to God.* For our sake He made Him to be sin who knew no sin, so that in Him we might become the righteousness of God. (Italics added.)

This concept of reconciliation to God sets this carol apart from many of the others, thus displaying its rich theological content.

The only possible scriptural issues with "Hark! The Herald Sing" is the lyric stating that the angels sang, "Glory to the newborn King!" Let's compare that to Luke 2:13, "And suddenly there was with the angel a multitude of the heavenly host praising God and saying, "Glory to God in the highest and on earth peace among those with whom He is pleased!" The angels did not specifically announce, "Glory to the newborn King." However, they were praising God at the occasion of Christ's birth. Since Christ is fully God, it is not antithetical to summarize the angel's proclamation as "Glory to the newborn King."

Overall, "Hark! The Herald Angels Sing" is a theologically rich Christmas hymn. It clearly presents the gospel and promotes reconciliation between a perfect God and sinful man. The richness of the lyrics and joyful refrain make this song one that should be sung every holiday season.

In the Bleak Midwinter

In the bleak mid - win - ter, fros - ty wind made moan,
God, heav'n can - not hold Him, nor earth sus - tain;
Enough for Him, whom cher - ubim wor - ship night and day,
An - gels and arch - an - gels may have gath - ered there,
What can I give Him, poor as I am?

earth stood hard as i - ron, wa - ter like a stone;
heav'n and earth shall flee a - way when He comes to reign.
A breast - ful of milk, and a man - ger - ful of hay:
Cher - u - bim and ser - a - phim throng - ed the air.
If I were a shep - herd, I would bring a lamb.

snow had fal - len, snow on snow snow on snow,
In the bleak mid - win - ter a sta - ble place suf - ficed the
Enough for Him whose an - gels fall down be - fore,
But His moth - er on - ly, in her maid - en bliss,
If I were a wise man, I would do my part,

in the bleak mid - win - ter long a - go. 2.Our
Lord God Al - might - y Je - sus Christ.
th'ox and ass and ca - mel which a - dore.
wor - shipped the Be - lov - ed, with a kiss.
What can I give Him? Give Him my heart.

Lyrics: Christina Rossetti
Music: Gustav Holst
Arr. Timothy Mulder, 2025

11

In the Bleak Midwinter

———◦———◦———

LUKE 2:13-14

*And suddenly there was with the angel a multitude of the
heavenly host praising God and saying,
"Glory to God in the highest, and on earth
peace among those with whom he is pleased!"*

CHOIRMASTERS CONSIDER "IN THE BLEAK Midwinter" the greatest Christmas carol ever.[42] The lyrics are based on a poem by English poet Christina Rossetti, which was published in the January 1872 issue of *Scribner's Monthly*. Thirty-five years later, Gustav Holst set those lyrics to his hymn, "Cranham". Shortly

---

[42] https://www.wqxr.org/story/176280-five-greatest-carols-ever/ Accessed March 31, 2025.

thereafter, it was published in the *English Hymnal*. Its hauntingly beautiful melody and harmony has made it a favorite carol ever since.

Lyricist Christina Rossetti was born in England to Italian immigrants. Her Anglican mother home-schooled her, and she declined two marriage proposals due to theological disputes with her suitors. She remained single her entire life, serving God by ministering to former prostitutes and working with the *Society for Promoting Christian Knowledge*. The Society was, and still is, an English charity that aims to raise awareness of the Christian faith in England and worldwide.

The opening stanza describes a winter scene in which the earth is frozen and snow is falling. Some claim that Rossetti described the weather in Bethlehem that first Christmas night. However, at that time of year, Judea is typically warm, and the first stanza of the carol does not match the climate there. John Mulder and F. Morgan Roberts, in their book *28 Carols to Sing at Christmas*, note that "Although not unheard of, snow in Palestine is rare."[43] Additionally, Rossetti wrote during the time when literary works such as Dickens' *A Christmas Carol* had established a strong association between the Christmas season and snowy weather.

In the second verse, Rossetti contrasts Jesus' second coming with His first. The first line speaks of heaven and earth not being able to contain or sustain God. 1 Kings 8:27 asks and answers the question, "But will God indeed dwell on the earth? Behold, heaven and the highest heaven cannot contain you; how much less this house that I have built!" Therefore, the first line of the second stanza of the carol is scriptural. Heaven cannot contain our amazing God.

What about Rossetti's next statement that "heaven and earth shall flee away?" The answer for this lies in Revelation 21:1, where the Apostle John says, "Then I saw a new heaven and a new earth, for the first heaven and the first earth had passed away, and the sea was no more." So, while the carol's second stanza may not seem biblical, we can rest assured that it is.

The carol's third stanza focuses on the birth of Jesus and the humble circumstances surrounding it. The third and fourth stanzas mention cherubim and seraphim, which are not specifically mentioned as being at Christ's birth. The fourth stanza contrasts the angels' mighty presence at Jesus' birth and the

---

[43] John M. Mulder and F. Morgan Roberts, *28 Carols to Sing at Christmas.* (Eugene: Wipf and Stock, 2015), 66.

newborn Jesus's intimate relationship with His mother. The carol also refers to archangels in the plural, while Scripture lists only one, Michael.[44]

There is a major theological issue with the line, "Angels and archangels *may* have gathered there." (Italics added.) For the Bible-believing Christian, the word "may" is offensive. Scripture says that the angels gathered and proclaimed the birth of the Son of God.[45] If we truly consider the Bible to be God's inerrant Word, we will not question whether or not the angels were present. We know beyond the shadow of a doubt that angels were there. So, to say that they *may* have been there casts doubt on the inerrancy of Scripture.

The carol's final stanza shifts from the glory of the angels and the humility of the manger to a personal, introspective thought about what those listening to the carol can give to the Almighty King, who humbled Himself and was born a pauper. The stanza speaks of the gifts of the shepherds and the wise men. Scripture does not indicate that the shepherds gave Jesus any gifts, let alone a lamb. However, the stanza looks at it from a personal perspective, with the vocalist making a hypothetical statement that if they were a shepherd, they would bring a lamb. The final line of the fifth stanza speaks of the gift that we all can bring Him, which is our hearts.

As we near the celebration of Christ's first coming and look forward to the glory of His second coming, let us remember that in the meantime, we are to bring Him our hearts.

---

[44] Jude 9, "But when the archangel Michael, contending with the devil, was disputing about the body of Moses, he did not presume to pronounce a blasphemous judgment, but said, "The Lord rebuke you."

[45] Luke 2:13-14, "And suddenly there was with the angel a multitude of the heavenly host praising God and saying, 'Glory to God in the highest, and on earth peace among those with whom he is pleased!'"

Infant Holy, Infant Lowly

1. In - fant ho - ly, in - fant low - ly for His bed a cat - tle stall; Ox - en
2. Flocks were sleep - ing, shep-herds keep-ing vi - gil 'til the mor-ning new; Saw the

low - ing, lit - tle know - ing Christ, the Babe is Lord of all. Swift are
glo - ry, heard the sto - ry ti - dings of a gos-pel true. Thus re -

wing - ing an - gels sing - ing, No-els ring - ing, ti - dings bring - ing, Christ, the
joi - cing, free from sor - row, Prai-ses voi - cing, meet the mor - row, Christ, the

Babe is Lord of all. Christ the Babe is Lord of all.
Babe was born for you. Christ the Babe was born for you.

Traditional Polish Carol
Arr. Timothy Mulder, 2025

12

Infant Holy, Infant Lowly

———⟨❧⟩———

REVELATION 17:14B

He is Lord of lords and King of kings, and those with Him are called and chosen and faithful.

NOT MUCH IS KNOWN ABOUT the history of "Infant Holy, Infant Lowly". We do know that it is a traditional Polish Christmas carol dating back to the thirteenth century. The carol is known in Polish as *W Żłobie Leży*, or "In the Manger He Lies." The song's musical form is a polonaise, a Polish national dance popularized by Frédéric Chopin.

Lyrically, the carol is solidly biblical. The theme of the carol's first stanza is that "Christ the Babe is Lord of all." The carol begins with the holy baby Jesus sleeping in a cattle stall. While Jesus was likely born in a cattle stall,

Scripture is clear that His bed was a manger. The word manger comes from the Latin word meaning "to chew." It refers to the trough where cattle ate. The word also appears in Luke 2 three times, in verses 7, 12, and 16. In Scripture, when words are repeated, they are frequently done to emphasize a point.[46] This repetition tells us that the manger is very important. We are to pay attention to it as we read the Christmas story.

According to Luke 2:7,[47] Mary laid her baby boy in "a manger, because there was no place for them in the inn." This was no accident. God planned for Jesus to be born in humble, dirty surroundings. If you've ever been around cattle, you know that they are not the cleanest of animals. Usually, there is a stench of manure around them. They get muddy, wet, and smelly. We would never allow a dirty, stinky bull into a hospital, let alone the part of the hospital where babies are born. And yet, that is precisely where the newborn Jesus, the holy Son of God, was. He was laid in the trough where those dirty animals were fed. By having His Son lie in a manger, God showed us how much Jesus had humbled Himself to come to earth.

Luke 2:11-12 tells us that the manger was a sign for the shepherds, "For unto you is born this day in the city of David a Savior, who is Christ the Lord. And this will be a sign for you: you will find a baby wrapped in swaddling cloths and lying in a manger." The angels told the shepherds that Jesus was born and that the way that they would be able to identify Him was that He was wrapped in swaddling cloths and lying in a manger. All babies are wrapped in swaddling cloths. But this baby was different. He was lying in a manger. The manger was the sign that Jesus was the Son of God. He was the one of whose birth the angels proclaimed. And, according to Luke 2:16,[48] the shepherds found "Mary and Joseph, and the baby lying in a manger."

Returning to the first stanza of the carol, the oxen were lowing around the cattle stall where Jesus was lying in the manger.[49] The next line of the carol tells us what the sign of the manger revealed: Christ the Babe is Lord of all.

---

[46] For example, in Revelation 4:8, the Apostle John says that the angels around the throne were repeating, "Holy, holy, holy, is the Lord God Almighty, who was and is and is to come!" The angels were not simply saying that God is holy. They were saying that God is really, really holy!"
[47] Luke 2:7, "And she gave birth to her firstborn son and wrapped Him in swaddling cloths and laid Him in a manger, because there was no place for them in the inn."
[48] Luke 2:16, "And they went with haste and found Mary and Joseph, and the baby lying in a manger."
[49] Imagine trying to lay your baby boy down for a nap, and the animals are lowing and mooing, keeping him awake. A stable is no place for a newborn.

Lying in a dirty feed trough, this tiny human child is Lord of all. He is *not going to be* Lord of all. He already is!

The stanza moves on to the angels singing about the birth. The next line says that "noels" were ringing. What is a noel? We sing about them each Christmas when we sing "The First Noel." A noel is an exclamation or proclamation. So when we sing about the first Noel, we sing about the angels' proclamation that very first Christmas.

The second stanza of "Infant Holy, Infant Lowly" continues with the theme of the humility of Jesus Christ. The shepherds' flocks were sleeping on the Judean mountainsides. The shepherds were there, keeping vigil throughout the night. They had seen the glory of God revealed to them by the angelic host. When they journeyed to the manger, they witnessed the true gospel. They had witnessed the human manifestation of Emmanuel, God with us. This Emmanuel would free us from the sorrow of sin and pain and death and suffering. This newborn child, holy and lowly, would turn everything back to the way that it was before sin entered the world.

Our response to Christ restoring this world to how it was meant to be should be nothing short of exclamatory praise to the One who has saved us. Our songs should "greet the morrow," as the carol says. They should ring out throughout the night as we celebrate the One who was born to die so that we might live. Who is that One? The carol tells us one last time. It is Christ the Babe, born for you.

It Came Upon the Midnight Clear

Edmund H. Sears, 1850
Arr. Timothy Mulder, 2025

13

It Came Upon the Midnight Clear

LUKE 2:13-14

*And suddenly there was with the angel a multitude of the
heavenly host praising God and saying,
"Glory to God in the highest,
and on earth peace among those with whom He is pleased!"*

"IT CAME UPON THE MIDNIGHT Clear" is the only Christmas carol in this book
that does not mention the birth of Jesus. The focus is on the message of the
angels, as found in Luke 2:14. The lyrics were written in poem form by

Unitarian[50] pastor Edmund Sears in 1849.[51] The following year, Richard Storrs Willis set the poem to his tune, "Carol." Sears wrote the poem just after the Mexican-American war. Perhaps the most notable of the five stanzas of the carol is the third, which focuses on 2,000 years of war. Today, most hymnals omit Sears' third verse, focusing the carol on the angels.

The carol's first stanza begins with the angels playing their harps. While Scripture does not say that the angels played harps, it does tell us that the twenty-four elders around the throne of God did. Revelation 5:8-9a tells us that "the twenty-four elders fell down before the Lamb, each holding a harp, and golden bowls full of incense, which are the prayers of the saints. And they sang a new song."

The next line of the stanza has the angels saying, "Peace on the earth, good will to men, from heaven's all gracious king." According to Luke 2:14,[52] the angels said, "Peace on earth among those with whom He is pleased." The recipients of the angels' proclamation are different in the carol than in Scripture. In the carol, peace is given to *all* men. In Luke 2:14, peace on earth is given to those *with whom God is pleased*. The carol's deviation from Scripture makes sense, given the author of the lyrics is Unitarian. Unitarians believe in universal salvation, which means that everyone is saved. Therefore, Unitarians interpret Luke 2:14 to say, "Peace on earth among all men," since God is pleased with all men. "A weary world" is a just description of the earth burdened with the sin of mankind and growing weary as it awaits the Messiah. Describing the plains as "sad and lowly" provides poetic juxtaposition for the exultation, light, and joy the message of the angels brings.

Left out of most hymnals, the third stanza begins with the world's suffering due to sin and strife. It says the world has suffered wrong for two thousand years since Jesus' birth.[53] The stanza speaks about how war covers up the love song the angels bring. It finishes with a command for mankind to be quiet and listen to the angels.

---

[50] The Unitarian church encourages its members to develop their own personal theology. Unitarians do not believe in one specific god but worship the god of their choosing. Unitarianism, as a historical movement, emerged from a rejection of the Christian doctrine of the Trinity (God as Father, Son, and Holy Spirit).

[51] It is ironic that a Unitarian wrote a Christmas Carol, since they believe all mankind is saved and Jesus may be worshiped, but assign to Him no value beyond that of a false god.

[52] Luke 2:14, "Glory to God in the highest, and on earth peace among *those with whom he is pleased!*" (Italics added.)

[53] However, according to Scripture, the world has suffered wrong since Adam and Eve committed the first sin in Genesis 3.

Stanza 4 speaks of "life's crushing load" and man's "bending low." The stanza focuses on the consequences of the fall, "with toil along the climbing way with painful steps and slow." But then the stanza suggests we focus on the angels, for "glad and golden hours" are coming, brought about by the angels singing. This stanza runs contrary to the gospel in that the true remedy to suffering in life is not the singing of heavenly beings, but the reason for their song, the Son of God, Himself. In Matthew 11:28-30, Jesus tells us, "Come to me, all who labor and are heavy laden, and I will give you rest. Take my yoke upon you, and learn from me, for I am gentle and lowly in heart, and you will find rest for your souls. For my yoke is easy, and my burden is light." The true remedy to the maladies of sin is not the music of the angels but the One who was born on Christmas, Jesus Christ. He has conquered sin and death; if we come to Him alone, we will find rest for our weary souls.

Stanza 5 speaks of the world rejoicing together with the angels. The days are passing, just as the prophets said they would. Eventually, according to stanza 5, peace will overtake the earth, and the whole earth will join the angels in their song. Sadly, the carol does not state how peace will come about. In fact, it makes no mention of Jesus at all. It speaks not of His birth nor of His second coming. Jesus, in John 16:33, tells us where peace truly comes from, "I have said these things to you, that *in me* you may have peace. In the world, you will have tribulation. But take heart; I have overcome the world." (Italics added.) Peace does not come from angels. Nor does it come from the world. The world only brings about trials, tribulations, and death. True peace only comes from the One who has conquered death and overcame the world: Jesus Christ. He is Emmanuel, God with us. And faith in Him is the only way to experience true peace. There is no other way.

While this carol is beautiful to sing, its theology is not biblical. Angels' songs do not bring us peace. The One of whom the angels sing is the One who brings us true peace. Let our focus be on Him alone this holiday season.

Joy to the World

Joy to the world! The Lord is come: let earth re - ceive her King; let
Joy to the earth! The Sav - ior reigns: let men their songs em - ploy; while
No more let sins or sor - rows grow, nor thorns in - fest the ground; He
He rules the world with truth and grace, and makes the na - tions prove the

e - very heart pre - pare Him room and heav'n and na - ture sing, and
fields and floods, rocks, hills, and plains re - peat the sound - ing joy, re -
comes to make His bles - sings flow, far as the curse is found, far
glo - ries of His right - eous - ness and won - ders of His love, and

heav'n and na - ture sing, and heaven, and heaven and na - ture sing.
peat the sound - ing joy, re - peat re - peat the sound - ing joy.
as the curse is found, far as, far as the curse is found.
won - ders of His love, and won - ders, won - ders of His love.

Isaac Watts, 1719
George Frederick Handel, 1742
Arr. Lowell Mason, 1836
Arr. Timothy Mulder, 2025

14

Joy to the World

PSALM 98:4

Make a joyful noise to the LORD, all the earth;
break forth into joyous song and sing praises!

The lyrics for "Joy to the World" were written by Isaac Watts in 1719. Like many young people today, Watts found the church's music boring and unjoyful. When he complained to his father, his father encouraged him to do something about it. This creative challenge resulted in Isaac Watts composing over six hundred hymns and poems. These included: "When I Survey the Wondrous Cross" and "This is the Day the Lord Has Made." Initially, Watts's hymns were met with contempt. At the time, no one wanted hymns that were summaries of Scripture. After some time, Watts became the pastor at Mark Lane Independent

Chapel in London. During this time, he wrote the poem "Joy to the World." The church began to sing the poem to the tune of "Come Thou Fount of Every Blessing."

Forty years after Isaac Watts's death, Lowell Mason was born in New Jersey. Mason was musically talented, eventually becoming a student of the composer Handel. Mason produced a book of original music and arrangements, but it was rejected by every publisher to whom he submitted it. Frustrated, he became the organist at a local Presbyterian church. However, a few years later, the Handel and Hayden Society of Massachusetts ordered fifty thousand copies of his songbook. Mason began to write music again, producing hymns such as "My Faith Looks Up to Thee" and "Nearer My God to Thee." He also wrote a piece called "Antioch," but he could not come up with words that fit the melody. Eventually, he began to read poetry, searching for something that would fit. He came across Isaac Watts's poem, "Joy to the World," and providentially, it fit with the melody of "Antioch." In 1911, popular singer Elise Stevenson joined Trinity Choir for a Christmas release of "Joy to the World." The song went to number five on the National Hit Parade, marking the first time that either Watts or Mason had a song on the charts. However, the song also inspired a rock music hit for Three Dog Night, which went to number one on the Billboard Music Charts in America.

Unlike most Christmas carols, "Joy to the World" is not based on Luke 2 but on Psalm 98, specifically verse 4.[54] According to Isaac Watts, that is the only specific verse upon which the carol is based. However, stanzas 2-4 each allude to a specific portion of Scripture and to the message of many carols; namely the incarnation of Jesus Christ who came to break the yoke of sin and will reign over the earth throughout all eternity. The focus of the carol is the overwhelming joy of that message. That is why it is so popular today.

The carol's first two stanzas are a call to praise God. We will join heaven and nature to worship our God with songs of praise. We know that the heavens praise God, but what about nature? Does nature praise God? Luke 19:39-40 says, "And some of the Pharisees in the crowd said to Him, "Teacher, rebuke your disciples." He answered, "I tell you, if these were silent, the very stones would cry out." Indeed, the very stones will cry out to God in songs of praise. Stones are not living beings, yet they will cry out in praise to God. How much more should living beings cry out to Him?

---

[54] Psalm 98:4, "Make a joyful noise to the LORD, all the earth; break forth into joyous song and sing praises!"

Stanza 3 says "No more let sins or sorrows grow, nor thorns infest the ground; He comes to make His blessings flow, far as the curse is found." This stanza refers to Genesis 3:17-18,[55] which discusses the curse which the earth is suffering due to man's sin. God has sent His only Son to dwell among us and bring salvation. Jesus' birth, life, death and resurrection extends God's blessing to all of mankind and of the earth to break the curse. This blessing will be found in every area of life under sin's grasp and through it the earth will be healed.

The carol's fourth stanza alludes to Philippians 2:10-11, "At the name of Jesus every knee should bow, in heaven and on earth and under the earth, and every tongue confess that Jesus Christ is Lord, to the glory of God the Father." Every knee will bow to Him. Every tongue will confess His righteousness and love.

When looking at the lyrics, we see that "Joy to the World" is not a Christmas carol, per se. It is a song praising God's glorious plan to redeem mankind and the earth from the curse of sin and the proclaiming Christ's Lordship over the earth. The only part related to Christmas is the phrase, "The Lord has come." The reason that it is associated with Christmas is that in 1911, Elise Stevenson included it on a Christmas album. However, it certainly is one of the most popular Christmas carols.

The message of the carol is joy. Christmastime is not always a time of joy for everyone and many people struggle with depression and anxiety during the holidays. "Joy to the World" contains the message that many of us need to hear during the holidays. Actually, it should be sung year-round, as it inspires a joy unparalleled by most of the music sung in the church today. This Christmas season, lift your voice in joyous praise to our Lord who has come.

---

[55] Genesis 3:17-18, "And to Adam He said, "Because you have listened to the voice of your wife and have eaten of the tree of which I commanded you, 'You shall not eat of it,' cursed is the ground because of you; in pain you shall eat of it all the days of your life; [18] thorns and thistles it shall bring forth for you; and you shall eat the plants of the field."

Let All Mortal Flesh Keep Silence

1 Let all mor - tal flesh keep si - lence, and with fear and
2 King of kings, yet born of Ma - ry, as of old on
3 Rank on rank the host of hea - ven spreads its van - guard
4 At His feet the six winged ser - aph; cher - u - bim, with

trem - bling stand; pon - der noth - ing earth - ly min - ded,
earth He stood, Lord of lords, in hu - man ves - ture,
on the way, as the Light of light des - cend - eth
sleep - less eye, veil their fac - es to the pres - ence,

for with bles - sing in His hand, Christ our God to
in the bo - dy and the blood, He will give to
from the realms of end - less day, that the powers of
as with cease - less voice they cry, "Al - le - lu - ia,

earth des - cend - eth, our full ho - mage to de - mand.
all the faith - ful His own self for heaven - ly food.
hell may va - nish as the dark - ness clears a - way.
al - le - lu - ia, al - le - lu - ia Lord most high."

Liturgy of St. James, 5th century
Arr. Ralph Vaughan Williams, 1906
Arr. Timothy Mulder, 2025

15

Let All Mortal Flesh Keep Silence

HABAKKUK 2:20

But the LORD is in His holy temple; let all the earth keep silence before Him.

"LET ALL MORTAL FLESH KEEP Silence" is based on the "Prayer of the Cherubic Hymn," dating back to the 4th century. The Greek text is found in the *Liturgy of St. James*, which was initially credited to James the Lesser, one of the twelve disciples. However, more recently, hymnologists agree that it was created by Cyril of Jerusalem in 347. In the *Liturgy of St James*, the "Prayer of the Cherubic Hymn" was chanted as the bread and wine were brought into the sanctuary. The text is based on Habakkuk 2:20 and Zechariah 2:13.[56] The music for the carol comes from a book of French folk songs, *Chansons Populaires des Provinces de France,* published in 1860. In 1906, English composer Ralph Vaughan Williams paired it with this text for the English Hymnal, and that is the version we know and love today.

The carol is lyrically connected to Revelation 4:8[57] and Isaiah 6:3,[58]in which the six-winged angels cry, "Holy, holy, holy is the LORD of hosts; the whole earth is full of His glory!" The somber carol invites the singer to participate in the mystery of the incarnation.[59]

The carol opens with the command to be silent and stand with fear and trembling as we contemplate Christ's incarnation. Christ's humility in coming to earth and becoming a servant, even to the point of death on a cross, demands nothing less than our fullest reverence and allegiance. The almighty God of heaven, the world's Creator, humbled Himself and walked among His creation.

The carol's second stanza emphasizes the dichotomy between the glory of the King of kings and the humble circumstances surrounding His birth. He is Lord of lords and yet appeared in human skin. He had a physical body and blood, which He gave to the faithful the night He was crucified. The final line in the second stanza concludes, "He will give to all the faithful His own self for heavenly food." The line is reminiscent of John 6:51, "I am the living bread that came down from heaven. If anyone eats this bread, he will live forever. And the bread that I will give for the life of the world is my flesh." John 6:52-58[60] provides more detail and emphasizes what it means for Jesus to give Himself for heavenly food."

---

[56] Zechariah 2:13, "Be silent, all flesh, before the LORD, for He has roused Himself from His holy dwelling."

[57] Revelation 4:8, "And the four living creatures, each of them with six wings, are full of eyes all around and within, and day and night they never cease to say, 'Holy, holy, holy, is the Lord God Almighty, who was and is and is to come!'"

[58] Isaiah 6:2-3, "Above him stood the seraphim. Each had six wings: with two he covered his face, and with two he covered his feet, and with two he flew. [3] And one called to another and said: 'Holy, holy, holy is the LORD of hosts; the whole earth is full of His glory!'"

[59] https://www.umcdiscipleship.org/resources/history-of-hymns-let-all-mortal-flesh-keep-silence-1 Accessed April 3, 2025

[60] John 6:52-58, "The Jews then disputed among themselves, saying, "How can this man give us His flesh to eat?" [53] So Jesus said to them, "Truly, truly, I say to you, unless you eat the flesh of the Son of Man and drink His blood, you have no life in you. [54] Whoever feeds on my flesh and drinks my blood has eternal life, and I will raise him up on the last day. [55] For my flesh is true food, and my blood is true drink. [56] Whoever feeds on my flesh and drinks my blood abides in me, and I in him. [57] As the living Father sent me, and I live because of the Father, so whoever

The carol's third stanza echoes the Nicene Creed with images of "Light of light descending."[61] The Light of light, Jesus Christ, has descended from the realms of heaven, the place where there is no darkness because Christ is the light. Because Christ, in all His glory, lights up eternity, the powers of hell will vanish with the shadows. There is no question that this will happen. We can trust that what God has said will come about is going to happen.

The carol's final stanza alludes to Revelation 4:8, which reads, "And the four living creatures, each of them with six wings, are full of eyes all around and within, and day and night they never cease to say, "Holy, holy, holy, is the Lord God Almighty, who was and is and is to come!" The hymn writers have taken some artistic license and deviated from Scripture, in that the angels in Revelation 4:8 cried "holy, holy, holy is the Lord God Almighty," while the angels in the carol cry, "alleluia, alleluia, alleluia, Lord, most high." Holy means to be set apart. Alleluia means "praise be to God."

This Christmas season, let us join the angels in praising Emmanuel, the Son of God who has humbled Himself and came to live among us, His creation. Indeed, all of God's creation will one day offer Him the same praise that the angels did, whether it be "holy, holy, holy" or "alleluia, alleluia, alleluia." Our praises will be raised to His glorious throne.

---

feeds on me, he also will live because of me. [58] This is the bread that came down from heaven, not like the bread the fathers ate, and died. Whoever feeds on this bread will live forever."

[61] Revelation 21:23, "And the city has no need of sun or moon to shine on it, for the glory of God gives it light, and its lamp is the Lamb."

Lo, How a Rose E'er Blooming

1. Lo, how a Rose e'er bloom - ing From ten - der stem
2. I - sa - iah 'twas fore - told it, The Rose I have
3. The shep - herds heard the sto - ry, pro - claimed by an -
4. The flow'r, whose fra - grance ten - der with sweet - ness fills
5. O Sav - ior, child of Ma - ry, who felt our hu -

hath sprung! Of Jes - se's lin - eage com - ing As
in mind: With Ma - ry we be - hold it, The
- gels bright, how Christ, the Lord of glo - ry, was
- the air, dis - pels with glo - rious splen - dor the
- man woe; O Sav - ior, King of glo - ry, who

men of old have sung. It came, a flow - er bright,
vir - gin moth - er kind. To show God's love a - right
born on earth this night. To Beth - le - hem they sped
dark - ness ev - 'ry where. True Man, yet ve - ry God;
dost our weak - ness know, bring us at length, we pray,

A - mid the cold of win - ter when half - gone was the night.
She bore to men a Sav - ior when half - gone was the night.
and in the man - ger found Him, as an - gel her - alds said.
from sin and death He saves us and light - ens ev - 'ry load.
to the bright courts of heav - en and to the end - less day.

German Hymn, 15th Century
Arr. Michael Praetorius, 1609
Arr. Timothy Mulder, 2025

16

Lo, How a Rose E'er Blooming

ISAIAH 11:1

There shall come forth a shoot from the stump of Jesse,
and a branch from His roots shall bear fruit.

THE LYRICS FOR "LO HOW a Rose E'er Blooming" date back to 15th-century Germany. It first appeared in print as the poem, "Es ist ein Ros entsprungen,"[62] in 1582 and had 23 stanzas! Thankfully, today, it has been trimmed down to just five. The lyrics are based on two Old Testament passages: Song of Solomon

---

[62] Some have questioned the correct word in the first line of stanza one. Was the German word *ros* (rose) or *reis* (branch)?

2:1[63] and Isaiah 11:1.[64] Song of Solomon refers to the "rose of Sharon." The King James Version was the first translation to call it that. Prior to the King James Version, the words were translated "a flower of the field." The identity of the rose of Sharon is unclear and is disputed among scholars. The one thing they do agree on is that it is a flower, but not a rose.

The meaning of the carol changes based on whether you focus on Song of Solomon 2:1 or Isaiah 11:1. The Roman Catholic Church maintains that the verse from Song of Solomon refers to Mary, the mother of Jesus, as the rose of Sharon (without thorns).[65] The Protestant church has used Isaiah 11:1, which prophesies that Jesus is the "shoot from the stump of Jesse," as sung about in the first stanza.

The music for the carol was written by Michael Praetorius (1571-1621). Praetorius was a German composer who specialized in Protestant hymns. Originally, "Lo How a Rose E'er Blooming" was a twelfth-night carol sung on the last of the twelve days of Christmas. In recent years, the carol has been recorded by Percy Faith, Linda Ronstadt, Charlotte Church, and Sting.

The carol's first two stanzas speak of Old Testament prophecies concerning the birth of Jesus. The prophecy in Isaiah 11:1 is fulfilled in Jesus being from Jesse's lineage. This is supported by Matthew 1:2-16, which lists the genealogy of Jesus from Abraham. The line "As men of old have sung" refers to the people of the Old Testament who longed for a Savior. In fact, the Old Testament contains over 300 prophecies that have been fulfilled in Jesus Christ. The carol's first stanza then compares Jesus to a bright flower, who came in the cold of winter, in the middle of the night. Stanza 2 states that Isaiah prophesied about the flower of Jesus. He does so in Isaiah 9:2[66] and Isaiah 9:6,[67] although there are many other prophecies in Isaiah. Isaiah 7:14,[68] speaks of the virgin bearing a son. The rest of the carol's second stanza seems to indicate that Mary is not the rose because it says, "With Mary, we beheld it."

---

[63] Song of Solomon 2:1, "I am a rose of Sharon, a lily of the valleys."

[64] Isaiah 11:1, "There shall come forth a shoot from the stump of Jesse, and a branch from His roots shall bear fruit."

[65] After reading the carol's lyrics, one would be hard pressed to say the carol is about Mary.

[66] Isaiah 9:2, "The people who walked in darkness have seen a great light; those who dwelt in a land of deep darkness, on them has light shone.

[67] Isaiah 9:6, "For to us a child is born, to us a son is given; and the government shall be upon His shoulder, and His name shall be called Wonderful Counselor, Mighty God, Everlasting Father, Prince of Peace."

[68] Isaiah 7:14, "Therefore the LORD Himself will give you a sign. Behold, the virgin shall conceive and bear a son and shall call His name Emmanuel."

Stanza 3 shifts from prophecy to telling the story of the shepherds and the angels as found in Luke 2:8-11.[69] The carol's fourth stanza returns to the flower metaphor, speaking of the flower filling the air with its sweetness and dispelling darkness. The stanza then references the second stanza of the Nicene Creed, which reads, "We believe in one Lord, Jesus Christ, the only Son of God, eternally begotten of the Father, God from God, Light from Light, *true God from true God*, begotten, not made, of one being with the Father." (Italics added.) The carol makes it abundantly clear that, although Jesus was 100% human, He was also 100% God. This is known as the "hypostatic union." Scriptural support for the hypostatic union of Jesus can be found in John 1:1[70] and Philippians 2:5-8,[71] among other verses. The carol's fourth stanza concludes with a concise summary of the gospel by telling us that Jesus is the one who saves mankind from sin and death.

The final stanza of the carol refers to the hypostatic union again. It tells us that Jesus is our Savior, the child of Mary and the King of Glory. That very same Jesus will ultimately save us and usher us into heaven to be with Him. "In the midst of our suffering, this carol reminds us of God's presence and deliverance; Jesus Christ is the ever-blooming rose."[72]

---

[69] Luke 2:8-11, "And in the same region there were shepherds out in the field, keeping watch over their flock by night. 9 And an angel of the Lord appeared to them, and the glory of the Lord shone around them, and they were filled with great fear. 10 And the angel said to them, 'Fear not, for behold, I bring you good news of great joy that will be for all the people. 11 For unto you is born this day in the city of David a Savior, who is Christ the Lord.'"

[70] John 1:1, "In the beginning was the Word, and the Word was with God, and the Word was God."

[71] Philippians 2:5-8, "Have this mind among yourselves, which is yours in Christ Jesus, 6 who, though He was in the form of God, did not count equality with God a thing to be grasped, 7 but emptied Himself, by taking the form of a servant, being born in the likeness of men. 8 And being found in human form, He humbled Himself by becoming obedient to the point of death, even death on a cross."

[72] Mulder and Roberts, 92.

O Come All Ye Faithful

1. O come, all ye faith - ful, joy - ful and tri - um - phant, O
2. Sing, choirs of an - gels, sing in ex - ul - ta - tion, O
3. Yea, Lord, we greet Thee, born this hap - py morn - ing,

come ye, O co - me ye to Be - th - le - hem; Come and be -
sing, all ye ci - ti - zens of he - av'n a - bove; Glo - ry to
Je - sus, to Th - ee be all gl - o - ry giv'n; Word of the

hold Him born the King of a - n-gels; O come, let us a - dore Him, O
God, all glo - ry in the hi - gh-est; O come, let us a - dore Him, O
Fa - ther, late in flesh ap - pear - ring;

come, let us a - dore Him O come, let us a - dore Him, Chr - ist, the Lord

Attr. to John Francis Wade, 1751
Arr. Timothy Mulder, 2025

17

O Come All Ye Faithful

———— ⚭ ————

LUKE 2:15

When the angels went away from them into heaven,
the shepherds said to one another,
"Let us go over to Bethlehem and see this thing that has happened,
which the Lord has made known to us."

"O COME ALL YE FAITHFUL" is one of the most popular Christmas carols ever. It has been sung in churches of all denominations for over two hundred years and in Catholic masses even longer. It is one of the few religious Christmas carols to land in the top ten of music sales, doing so three times! It has been translated into over 150 languages. Many call it the "greatest carol ever written." Oddly, the hymn's author was unknown until after World War II.

For centuries, it was thought that an unknown cleric from the Middle Ages wrote the carol. Another assumption was that Saint Bonaventura had written the lyrics. However, in 1947, English scholar Maurice Frost discovered seven transcripts of "O Come All Ye Faithful" written by hand and signed by an English Catholic priest named John Francis Wade. In 1745, Wade was forced to leave England due to conflict between the Catholic and Anglican churches. He settled in Douay, France, where he researched and identified historical church music, then carefully recorded it and preserved it for future generations. Not only did he preserve historical church music, but he distributed it to Catholic churches across Europe. In doing so, he reintroduced many forgotten songs to untold numbers of people across the continent. In addition to preserving historical music, Wade dabbled in composing hymns. In 1750, he composed the melody to "Adeste Fideles," and about a decade later, he put lyrics to the melody.

In America and worldwide, "O Come All Ye Faithful" was adopted by many Christian churches before 1900. It gained popularity by becoming the focal point of the caroling movement that swept the country. The song became even more popular during the 1905 Christmas season when the Peerless Quartet, one of the most prominent vocal groups of the time, recorded and released the carol. Thousands of copies of the single were sold. The carol hit number 7 on the "National Hit Parade." Different versions of the carol appeared in the top 10 throughout the years. It was considered the nation's favorite Christmas song until Bing Crosby recorded "White Christmas" in 1954.

The theology presented in this carol is solidly scriptural. The chorus answers the first question of the Westminster Shorter Catechism, which asks, "What is the chief end of man?" The answer is "to glorify God and enjoy Him forever," as found in 1 Corinthians 10:31[73] and Psalm 73:28.[74] When we sing the carol, we repeat, "O come let us adore Him." When we adore God, we express deep love, reverence, and respect, worshiping Him for who He is and what He does. Our adoration is a response to God's love, acknowledging Him as Lord, and giving Him the glory and honor due His name. This is why we

---

[73] 1 Corinthians 10:31, "So, whether you eat or drink, or whatever you do, do all to the glory of God."

[74] Psalm 73:28, "But for me it is good to be near God; I have made the LORD GOD my refuge, that I may tell of all your works."

have been placed on this earth– to adore God. We are to come near to Him and adore Him.

"O Come All Ye Faithful" provides several different names for Jesus. The last line of the first stanza instructs us to "Come and behold Him, born the King of angels." Is Jesus truly the King of angels? For the answer, let's turn to Hebrews 1:6, which says, "And again, when He brings the firstborn into the world, He says, 'Let all God's angels worship Him.'" By stating that Christ is the King of angels, the author states that Jesus is exalted over all the angels through the union of His human nature with the divinity. Because His humanity is perfect, He is the Head and King of the angels even during His time on earth.

The second name for Jesus appears at the end of the chorus: Christ the Lord. The Scripture reference for this name is in Luke 2:11, "For unto you is born this day in the city of David a Savior, who is Christ the Lord." Christ comes from the Greek Word *Christos*, which means "anointed one" or "chosen one." "Lord" (with lower-case "ord") refers to Jesus, God, or "Adonai" in the Greek. This title emphasizes Jesus' lordship. This is the word that was used in Luke 2:11. This differs from "LORD," (all capitals) which refers to Yahweh or Jehovah.

The last name for Jesus appears in the third verse: Word of the Father. This name of Jesus is found in John 1:1-5.[75] The Word is the communication of God the Father. The Word was both *with* God and *was* God. John describes the role of the Word in creation and as a source of light and life. He declares the Word was with God in the beginning, calling the Word "He." John then goes on to describe the Word as the "light of men," a known description of Jesus. We also know that "the Word" refers to Jesus because John used these verses as a herald for his gospel about Jesus.

In summary, "O Come All Ye Faithful" is a wonderful celebration of the person of Jesus Christ. This carol should be sung more frequently than only during the Christmas season.

---

[75] John 1:1-5, "In the beginning was the Word, and the Word was with God, and the Word was God. [2] He was in the beginning with God. [3] All things were made through Him, and without Him was not anything made that was made. [4] In Him was life, and the life was the light of men. [5] The light shines in the darkness, and the darkness has not overcome it."

O Come, O Come, Emmanuel

1.O come, O come, Em – man – u – el, and ran – som cap – tive
2.O come, O come, Thou Lord of might, who to your tribes, on
3.O come, O Rod of Jes – se, free Thine own from Sa – tans
4.O come, Thou Day – spring from on high, and cheer us by Thy
5.O come, thou Key of Da – vid, come and o – pen wide our

Is – ra – el, that mourns in lone – ly ex – ile here, un –
Si – nai's height, in an – cient times did give the law in
ty – ra – ny; From depths of hell Thy peo – ple save and
draw – ing nigh; dis – perse the gloo – my clouds of night, and
heav'n – ly home; make safe the way that leads on high, and

til the Son of God ap – pear.
cloud and maj – es – ty and awe.
give them vic – t'ry o'r the grave.   Re – joice! Re – joice! Em
death's dark shad – ows put to flight.
close the path to mis – er – y.

man – u – el shall come to you, O Is – ra – el.

Latin Antiphons, 12th Century
Arr. Timothy Mulder, 2025

18

O Come, O Come, Emmanuel

ISAIAH 59:20

"And a Redeemer will come to Zion, to those in Jacob who turn from transgression," declares the LORD.

DATING BACK TO THE NINTH century, "O Come, O Come Emmanuel"[76] is the oldest Christmas carol sung today. It was originally sung as Gregorian chant and was used only in formal Catholic masses. The carol initially brought the story of Christ the Savior to life during the Dark and Middle Ages. For the illiterate people in the Middle Ages, the song provided the full story of how the

---

[76] The names Emmanuel and Immanuel both mean "God with us." The difference is that Immanuel is translated from the Hebrew and is used primarily in the Old Testament. Emmanuel is translated from the Greek and is used in the New Testament.

Old and New Testament views of the Messiah came together in the birth of Jesus. Because of this, many theologians consider it one of the most important songs of the Christian faith. In the fifteenth century, the carol was set to the melody we sing today. The carol contains five stanzas, each containing a different prophetical name for the Messiah. One stanza was sung weekly during Advent until Christmas Day when all five stanzas were sung. "O Come, O Come, Emmanuel" has been adopted and embraced by every major Christian denomination worldwide.

The carol became popular in the 19th century due to an Anglican priest named John Mason Neale, serving in the Madeira Islands off the northwest coast of Africa. He discovered it in a book of Latin hymns and translated the words into English, beginning with the lyrics, "Draw nigh, draw nigh, Emmanuel." Neale's version of the carol was published in the 1850s in England, and within 25 years, it was renamed "O Come, O Come, Emmanuel."

The carol's lyrics paint a rich illustration of the many biblical prophesies fulfilled by Christ's birth. Overall, the song reveals the unfolding story of the Messiah. The first stanza contains the name "Emmanuel," which is based on Isaiah 7:14[77] and Matthew 1:23.[78] The name Emmanuel means "God with us," which perfectly defines the person of Christ. He was God in human form, who came to dwell with His creation.

The second name for Jesus, found in the second stanza of the carol, is "Lord of Might," and this is based on Isaiah 9:6.[79] This title is critical, because if Jesus were not mighty, He would not have been able to rise from the dead. And that was the primary purpose of His life – to give us victory over death. The third stanza refers to Jesus as the "Rod of Jesse," which is based on Isaiah 11:1.[80] This name is important because it fulfills God's promise to David in 2 Samuel 7:16.[81] Here we see that Christ's throne will be established forever because He is of the branch of Jesse.

---

[77] Isaiah 7:14, "Therefore the LORD Himself will give you a sign. Behold, the virgin shall conceive and bear a son and shall call His name *Emmanuel.*" (Italics added.)

[78] Matthew 1:23, "Behold, the virgin shall conceive and bear a son and shall call His name *Emmanuel.*" (Italics added.)

[79] Isaiah 9:6, "For to us a child is born, to us a son is given; and the government shall be upon His shoulder, and His name shall be called Wonderful Counselor, *Mighty God,* Everlasting Father, Prince of Peace." (Italics added.)

[80] Isaiah 11:1, "There shall come forth a *shoot from the stump of Jesse,* and a branch from His roots shall bear fruit." (Italics added.)

[81] 2 Samuel 7:16, "And your house and your kingdom shall be made sure forever before me. Your throne shall be established forever."

The fourth stanza's name for Jesus is "Dayspring," which is based on Malachi 4:2[82] and Luke 1:78 (KJV).[83] "Dayspring" means the dawning of a new day. The new day is that of the law being fulfilled in Christ rather than relying upon the works of man. The last stanza calls Jesus the "Key of David," which is based on Isaiah 22:22.[84] A key indicates control or authority; therefore, having the Key of David would give one control of David's domain, (Jerusalem, the City of David, and the kingdom of Israel).

We sing about Emmanuel's ransoming of "captive Israel." Did the author refer only to the nation of Israel? This is not likely, as Israel is symbolic of the Christian church, held captive on a dark and sinful earth. Therefore, when we sing "ransom captive Israel," we are not talking about Israel as a nation but rather spiritual Israel – the Christian church. Biblical support for this can be found in Romans 9:6, which reads, "But it is not as though the Word of God has failed. For not all who are descended from Israel are a part of Israel," meaning that not all genetic Israelites are spiritual Israelites. Gentiles are now included in spiritual Israel. Salvation has come to the Gentiles! The inclusion of Gentiles in the new Israel, or Christian church, is a fundamental concept in Scripture because it shows that many of the promises made to Israel apply to the church.

"O Come, O Come, Emmanuel" is a solidly biblical hymn that shows how Old Testament prophecies were fulfilled in the person of Christ. This carol shows us that Jesus Christ truly is Emmanuel—He is God with us.

---

[82] Malachi 4:2, "But for you who fear my name, the *sun of righteousness shall rise* with healing in its wings. You shall go out leaping like calves from the stall." (Italics added.) (Note that this verse is referenced in Hark! The Herald Angels Sing, stanza 3.)

[83] Luke 1:78 (KJV), "Through the tender mercy of our God; whereby the *dayspring* from on high hath visited us." (Italics added.)

[84] Isaiah 22:22, "And I will place on His shoulder *the key of the house of David.* He shall open, and none shall shut; and He shall shut, and none shall open." (Italics added.)

O Holy Night

1.O Ho-ly Night! The stars are bright-ly shi - ning, It is the night of our
2.Led by the light of faith se-rene-ly beam - ing, With glow-ing hearts by His
3.Tru-ly He taught us love for one a - noth - er, His law is love and His

dear Sav-ior's birth Long lay the world in sin and er - ror pin-ning. Till He ap-
cra - dle we stand. O - ver the world a star is sweet-ly gleam - ing, Now come the
gos - pel is peace. Chains He shall break the slave is our broth - er, And in His name

peared and the soul felt it's worth. A thrill of hope the wea - ry world re - joi - ces, For
wise - men from O - ri - ent land. The King of kings lay thus in low - ly man - ger; In
all op - pres - sion shall cease. Sweet hymns of joy in grate - ful chor - us raise we, With

yon - der breaks a new and glor - ious morn. Fall_____ on your knees! Oh hear_____
all our tri - als born to be our friend. He_____ knows our need, Our weak -
all our hearts we praise His ho - ly name. Christ_____ is the Lord! Oh praise_____

_____ the an - gel voi - ces! O night_____ di - vine,_____ O_____ night_____ when Christ was
- ness is no strang - er! Be - hold_____ your King! Be - fore_____ Him low - ly
His name for - ev - er! His pow'r_____ and glo - ry_____ ev - er - more pro -

born;_____ O night,_____ O Ho - ly Night, O night di - vine!_____
bend!_____ Be - hold_____ your King!_____ Be - fore Him low - ly bend!
claim!_____ His pow'r_____ and glo - ry ev - er - more pro - claim!

Adolphe Charles Adams
Arr. Timothy Mulder, 2025

19

O Holy Night

LUKE 1:14

And you will have joy and gladness, and many will rejoice at His birth.

"O HOLY NIGHT" IS A wonderful carol in which the singer celebrates and worships the newborn baby Jesus. The song's climax is the last part of stanza 3, which proclaims, "Christ is the Lord! O praise His name forever!" What a glorious song of praise. However, the story behind the carol is riddled with legend and fact.

In 1843, a priest asked French wine merchant Placide Cappeau to write a Christmas poem to commemorate the renovation of the church's pipe organ. Once Cappeau had completed the poem "Cantique de Noel" (Song of Christmas), he asked Adolphe Adam to set it to music. The song debuted at a midnight mass on Christmas Eve, 1847. It rapidly became popular within the French church. That much we know as fact. The rest of the story is steeped in legend.

Cappeau was an atheistic socialist, and Adolphe Adam was Jewish. This became a problem for the Roman Catholic Church because, despite the hymn's beauty, it was written by authors who didn't celebrate the birth of Jesus. As a result, the Roman Catholic Church banned the carol for more than two decades. However, the Catholic Church's actions failed to diminish the song's popularity.

In 1855, "O Holy Night" was discovered by American abolitionist John Sullivan Dwight. The line in the third verse, "Chains He shall break; the slave is our brother, and in His name, all oppression shall cease," really moved him. Dwight translated the song from French into English and published it in his magazine, *Dwight's Journal of Music*. Due to its third verse, the carol became very popular in the Northern United States before the Civil War.

After 1871, the French Catholic Church allowed the song to be used in worship services due to a legendary encounter between French and German soldiers in the Franco-Prussian War. During a lull in the fighting on Christmas Eve, an unarmed French Soldier stepped out onto the battlefield and sang "Cantique de Noel." When he finished, the Germans responded by singing a German Christmas Carol. The truce lasted through Christmas Day.

Legend also states that "O Holy Night" was the first song to be broadcast live. A colleague of Thomas Edison, Reginald Fessenden, pioneered radio broadcasting. He had been working on using a microphone with a wireless telegraph. On Christmas Eve, 1906, Fessenden broadcast a recording of Handel's "Largo," followed by a reading of Luke 2, and then playing "O Holy Night" on the violin. Wireless operators on ships in the Atlantic Ocean were stunned to hear the first-ever AM radio broadcast. The carol has been played on radio stations around the world ever since. Notable renditions include those by Celine Dion, Josh Groban,[1] Mariah Carey, Lauren Daigle, and Martina McBride. In 1971, the Irish group Tommy Drennan and the Monarchs transformed the song into a number-one hit.

The carol begins by speaking of the most holy night: the night of the birth of Jesus. The sinful world surrounded Him, but in Him, there is a hope of relief from that sin. This line is based on 1 John 3:5, which reads, "You know that He

---

[1] Josh Groban's rendition has over 10 million views on YouTube!

appeared in order to take away sins, and in Him there is no sin." The chorus tells us to fall on our knees in worship because the One who will take away sin and suffering has been born.

The second stanza offers a parallel between the wise men seeking Jesus by following the star's light[2] and those of us who seek Him, who are led by the light of faith. Stanza two continues by presenting Jesus's humility and humanity. It speaks of Jesus as the King of kings. Yet, He is so humble that He is laid in a lowly manger.[3] Philippians 2:5-8[4] speaks of the humility of Christ, telling us that He was born in the likeness of men and further humbled Himself by becoming obedient to the point of death on the cross. And by being a man, Jesus is able to relate to us in our weaknesses.[5]

The third stanza speaks of Jesus teaching us how to love one another. It then speaks of the ending of oppression through Jesus Christ.[6] The final chorus of the carol is pure, unbridled praise, declaring that Christ is the Lord and we will praise His name forever. And that is what we are to do: declare Him as Lord and praise Him forever!

---

[2] Matthew 2:1-2, "Now after Jesus was born in Bethlehem of Judea in the days of Herod the king, behold, wise men from the east came to Jerusalem, [2] saying, "Where is He who has been born king of the Jews? For we saw His star when it rose and have come to worship Him."

[3] Luke 2:7, "And she gave birth to her firstborn son and wrapped Him in swaddling cloths and laid Him in a manger, because there was no place for them in the inn."

[4] Philippians 2:5-8, "Have this mind among yourselves, which is yours in Christ Jesus, [6] who, though He was in the form of God, did not count equality with God a thing to be grasped, [7] but emptied Himself, by taking the form of a servant, being born in the likeness of men. [8] And being found in human form, He humbled Himself by becoming obedient to the point of death, even death on a cross."

[5] 2 Corinthians 12:9, "But He said to me, 'My grace is sufficient for you, for my power is made perfect in weakness.' Therefore, I will boast all the more gladly of my weaknesses, so that the power of Christ may rest upon me."

[6] Luke 4:18-19, "The Spirit of the Lord is upon me, because He has anointed me to proclaim good news to the poor. He has sent me to proclaim liberty to the captives and recovering of sight to the blind, to set at liberty those who are oppressed, [19] to proclaim the year of the Lord's favor."

O Little Town of Bethlehem

1. O lit - tle town of Beth - le - hem, how still we see thee lie; a -
2. For Christ is born of Mar - ry; and gath-ered all a - bove, while
3. How si - lent - ly, how si - lent - ly, the won-drous gift is giv'n! So
4. O ho - ly child of Beth - le - hem, de - scend to us we pray; cast

bove thy deep and dream - less sleep, the si - lent stars go by: yet
mor - tals sleep, the an - gels keep their watch of won-d'ring love. O
God im - parts to hu - man hearts the bless - ings of His heav'n. No
out our sin and en - ter in; be born in us to - day. We

in thy dark streets shi - neth the ev - er - last - ing light; the
morn - ing stars, to - geth - er pro - claim the ho - ly birth! And
ear my hear his com - ing, but in this world of sin, where
hear the Christ - mas an - gels the great glad ti - dings tell; O

hopes and fears of all the years are met in thee to - night.
prais - es sing to God the King, and peace to men on earth.
meek souls will re - ceive Him still, the dear Christ en - ters in.
come to us, a - bide with us, our Lord Em - man - u - el.

Phillips Brooks, 1868
Arr. Timothy Mulder, 2025

20

O Little Town of Bethlehem

—————◦◦◦—————

Micah 5:2

But you, O Bethlehem Ephrathah, who are too little to be among the clans of Judah, from you shall come forth for me one who is to be ruler in Israel, whose coming forth is from of old, from ancient days.

"O Little Town of Bethlehem" is a beautiful, somber Christmas carol that conveys the beauty and stillness of the small town where Christ was born so long ago. And yet, the silence was broken by an event that would change the world. The holy child of Bethlehem was born to abide with us and take our sins as His own, assuring that we might spend eternity with Him.

Phillip Brooks pastored Holy Trinity Church in Philadelphia through the Civil War and gave the funeral message at President Abraham Lincoln's funeral in 1865. Burned out and exhausted from the war and its aftermath, Brooks took a sabbatical and traveled to the Holy Land. On Christmas Eve, he went by horseback from Jerusalem to Bethlehem. Along the way, he stopped at the "shepherds' fields," where it is believed that the angels announced the birth of Jesus to the shepherds. After pausing there, he came to Bethlehem where he worshiped at the Church of the Nativity, which is located near where it is believed that Jesus was born. The church rang with songs of praise late into the night. The experience refreshed Brooks, and upon his return home, he sought a way to convey those amazing moments to his congregation.

In 1868, Brooks finally wrote his thoughts on Bethlehem in poetic form. He then shared the poem with his church's organist, Lewis Redner. The organist labored for days to devise a suitable melody, desperately trying to complete the music by the December 24 deadline that Brooks had imposed. During the evening of December 24, the tune came to him. Brooks and Redner gathered a small choir and taught them the piece, which debuted on Christmas Day, 1868. It began to be sung around Philadelphia, but it wasn't until it was included in several collections of church music that it gained national popularity. Interestingly, in Great Britain, the song is not sung to Redner's tune but to the tune of "Forest Green" by Ralph Vaughn Williams.

The carol's lyrics do not seek to retell the Christmas story as found in Luke 2. Rather, they are a verbal snapshot of Bethlehem that first Christmas morning. The town was deep in sleep underneath the silent stars. And yet, in a manger within the city, shone a light brighter than the stars: the everlasting Light. And in the key line of the carol, in that everlasting Light, the "hopes and fears of all the years are met in Thee tonight."[7] Everything that man had longed for, since the fall of mankind back in Genesis 3, had finally been answered on that night. Sin, suffering, and death had a grip on the world, but now, One had come who would break that grip and provide God's people with hope. This concept is based on Revelation 21:4, "He will wipe away every tear from their eyes, and death shall be no more, neither shall there be mourning, nor crying, nor pain anymore, for the former things have passed away." The birth of Jesus was the beginning of the process of the removal of mourning, crying, and pain!

The lyrics in the second stanza speak of two different heavenly bodies: the angels, who are keeping their watch over Mary's newborn child, and the

---

[7] Colossians 1:27, "To them God chose to make known how great among the Gentiles are the riches of the glory of this mystery, which is Christ in you, the hope of glory."

morning stars, who proclaim Christ's birth and praise God the King, who will bring peace to mankind.

The third stanza speaks of the indwelling of the Holy Spirit. Unlike the arrival of Christ, which angels heralded, the Holy Spirit is silently imparted into human hearts. There is indeed praise when the Holy Spirit enters each heart. That praise, however, does not take place on earth but in heaven, where "there is joy before the angels of God over one sinner who repents."[8] The angels celebrate the indwelling of the Holy Spirit in each of God's chosen people. The presence of God brings with it the blessings of His heaven. According to Job 10:12,[9] the blessings of His heaven are eternal life, God's steadfast love, and God's care for His people. God has given these blessings to each person who has received the wondrous gift of the Holy Spirit. Psalm 8:4 says, "What is man that you are mindful of him, and the son of man that you care for him?" The universe is infinite in size; in comparison, man is only a speck on a tiny planet. But none of that matters to God. He made us, loves us, and is mindful of us.

The fourth stanza reiterates the theme of the third stanza by asking Jesus to cast out the sin in our hearts and enter in. That way, we, like the Christmas angels, might be able to spread the good news (glad tidings) about Emmanuel – God with us. This carol is a reminder of the peace and light brought into the world by the birth of our Savior, a message brought about by the depths of suffering wrought from war. Its message is as needed now as much as it was then. Let us go forth and share those glad tidings with a hurting world.

---

[8] Luke 15:10, "Just so, I tell you, there is joy before the angels of God over one sinner who repents."

[9] Job 10:12, "You have granted me life and steadfast love, and your care has preserved my spirit."

On Christmas Night (Sussex Carol)

1. On Christ - mas night all Chris - tians sing to hear the news___ the
2. Then why should men on earth___ be sad, since our Re - dee - mer
3. When sin de - parts be - fore___ Your grace, then life and health___ come
4. All out of dark - ness we___ have light, which made the an - gels

an - gels bring; on Christ - mas night all Chris - tians sing to
made us glad? Then why should men on earth___ be sad, since
in its place. When sin de - parts be - fore___ Your grace, then
sing this night; all out of dark - ness we___ have light, which

hear the news___ the an - gels bring: news of great joy,___ news of___ great
our Re - dee - mer made us glad, when from our sin___ he set___ us
life and health___ come in its place. An - gels and men___ with joy___ may
made the an - gels sing this night: "Glo - ry to God___ and peace___ to

mirth, news of our mer - ci - ful___ King's birth.
free, all for to gain our li - ber - ty.
sing, all for to see the new___ born King.
men, all now and for - e - ver - more.___ A - men."

Luke Wadding
Ralph Vaughan Williams and Harriet Verrall
Arr. Timothy Mulder, 2025

21

On Christmas Night (Sussex Carol)

LUKE 2:10

And the angel said to them, "Fear not, for behold,
I bring you good news of great joy that will be for all the people."

"ON CHRISTMAS NIGHT" IS ROOTED in both history and modernity. Though not well-known in the United States, the carol remains popular in the United Kingdom. The lyrics were first published in 1684 by Irish bishop Luke Wadding[10] in his collection of hymns, *A Smale [sic] Garland of Pious and Godly Songs Composed by a devout Man, For the Solace of his Freinds [sic]*

---

[10] The Wadding family lived in Wexford, famous for the Wexford Carol. The author of the Wexford Carol is unknown, although some suspect it may have been Bishop Wadding.

and neighbors in their afflictions. The text was titled, "Another short Carroll for Christmas Day." The carol and the songbook were meant to bring cheer to the Irish Catholics during the second half of the seventeenth century. They had undergone the British invasion of Ireland (1649-1653) under Oliver Cromwell, and entire cities were left in ruins.

Harriet Verrall sang the melody for the carol to Ralph Vaughan Williams near Monk's Gate, Sussex, England. (Hence the name "The Sussex Carol.") Williams took Harriet Verrall's melody and added the words to Bishop Wadding's hymn. He then published the carol in his 1919 book *Eight Traditional English Carols.*

The carol's lyrics do not retell the Christmas story like many other carols. Instead, it focuses on the theological ramifications of Jesus' birth. The first stanza begins with all Christians singing on Christmas night. They eagerly anticipate hearing the angels' proclamation of joy and mirth at the birth of Jesus. Ephesians 5:18-21[11] tells us that we are to sing "psalms and hymns and spiritual songs, singing and making melody to the Lord with your heart, giving thanks always and for everything to God the Father in the name of our Lord Jesus Christ." Psalm 95:1 also commands us to sing, "Oh come, let us sing to the LORD; let us make a joyful noise to the rock of our salvation!" When we gather together for worship, we are to sing thankfully and joyfully. Christmas is a special time of thankfulness and joy. It is the perfect time to gather together and sing to the Lord.

The carol's second stanza shifts away from the birth of Jesus to what He did on the cross. Stanza 2 tells us that the actions of Jesus Christ should make us glad because they have set us free from the slavery of sin. In Galatians 5:1, the apostle Paul tells us, "For freedom Christ has set us free; stand firm therefore, and do not submit again to a yoke of slavery." Before we were saved, each of us was a slave to sin. Sin had power over us. But the cross of Calvary and the empty tomb are evidence that we have been freed from slavery. Therefore, according to the verse's first line, men of earth should not be sad. That is not to say that we won't grieve certain things, but there should be an underlying joy that comes from the sacrifice of Christ.

---

[11] Ephesians 5:18-21, "And do not get drunk with wine, for that is debauchery, but be filled with the Spirit, [19] addressing one another in psalms and hymns and spiritual songs, singing and making melody to the Lord with your heart, [20] giving thanks always and for everything to God the Father in the name of our Lord Jesus Christ, [21] submitting to one another out of reverence for Christ."

Stanza 3 continues with the theological ramifications of Christ's incarnation, but then it returns to the manger scene in the last two lines. Before we were saved, every one of us was sinful.[12] However, now that the grace of Christ has saved us, that sin has vanished, and God sees us as His sinless children. Romans 5:20-21[13] tells us that where sin increased, grace abounded all the more. And that abounding grace leads to eternal life in Jesus Christ our Lord. The second line of stanza 2 says that life and health will come in the place of sin. This is true if we see it as happening after we physically die. While we are alive, we may have health problems, and we will die, but everlasting life is the result of Jesus' abounding grace. As such, we are to sing with the angels in abundant joy at the newborn King.

The final stanza begins by saying that Jesus is the light in the darkness. In John 8:12,[14] Jesus tells us that He is the light of the world. The carol finishes with a summary of the angels' proclamation at Jesus' birth, "Glory to God in the highest, and on earth peace among those with whom He is pleased!" We must be careful here because there is a difference between Scripture and the third line of the fourth verse. The carol says, "Peace to men," while the angels, according to Scripture, said, "peace among those with whom He is pleased." In the sacrifice of Jesus, God offers peace to His chosen people, not everyone. Not everyone will know the peace of God, so we must pray for them to come to know it.

---

[12] Romans 3:23, "for *all* have sinned and fall short of the glory of God." (Italics added.)

[13] Romans 5:20-21, "Now the law came in to increase the trespass, but where sin increased, grace abounded all the more, [21] so that, as sin reigned in death, grace also might reign through righteousness leading to eternal life through Jesus Christ our Lord."

[14] John 8:12, "Again Jesus spoke to them, saying, 'I am the light of the world. Whoever follows me will not walk in darkness but will have the light of life.'"

Once in Royal David's City

1 Once in ro - yal Da - vid's ci - ty stood a
2 He came down to earth from hea - ven, who is
3 And through all His won - drous - child - hood He would
4 And our eyes at last shall see Him, through His
5 Not in that poor low - ly sta - ble, with the

low - ly cat - tle shed, where a mo - ther laid her
God and Lord of all, and His shel - ter was a
ho - nour and o - bey, love and watch the low - ly
own re - deem - ing love; for that child, so dear and
ox - en stand - ing by, we shall see Him, but in

ba - by in a man - ger for his bed: Ma - ry
sta - ble, and His cra - dle was a stall: with the
mai - den, in whose gen - tle arms he lay; Christ - ian
gen - tle is our Lord in heav'n a bove; and He
heav - en, set at God's right hand on high; when like

was that mo - ther mild, Je - sus Christ her lit - tle child.
poor and meek and lowly lived on earth, our Sa - vior holy.
chil - dren all must be, mild, o - be - dient, good as He.
leads His child - ren on to the place where He is gone.
stars His child - ren crowned all in white shall wait a - round.

Cecil Frances Alexander, 1848
Arr. Timothy Mulder, 2025

22

Once In Royal David's City

LUKE 2:12

*And this will be a sign for you: you will find a baby
wrapped in swaddling cloths and lying in a manger.*

"ONCE IN ROYAL DAVID'S CITY" is a Christmas carol that emphasizes the
humility surrounding the birth of Jesus. "The carol's vivid text shatters
perceptions of the picturesque Nativity with the realities of the lowly stable,
and the weak and dependent baby."[15] Phrases such as "lowly cattle shed," "His
shelter was a stable and His cradle was a stall," and "poor, mean, and lowly"

[15] https://www.umcdiscipleship.org/resources/history-of-hymns-once-in-royal-davids-city-
serves-as-processional-hymn Accessed April 23, 2025.

bring Jesus' modest beginnings to life. The carol's final stanza shifts from humility to glorifying Christ when it speaks of Christ sitting at the right hand of God the Father.

In 1918, King's College in Cambridge began the Christmas tradition of the "Lessons and Carols"[16] service. In 1928, it was broadcast for the first time. Today, it is heard by millions of listeners around the world. In 1919, "Once in Royal David's City" was first used as the processional hymn for the service. A single choirboy sings the first verse. In each of the following stanzas, other vocalists, the whole choir, and the congregation join in singing together.

The author of the carol, Cecil Frances Alexander[17] was married to William Alexander, who became the archbishop of the Church of Ireland in Derry. In 1848, Mrs. Alexander published her music collection, *Hymns for Little Children*. "Once in Royal David's City" was included with other hymns to teach the Apostles' Creed poetically. This carol is based on the phrase "born of the Virgin Mary." Even though the song is considered a Christmas carol, it also describes Jesus as a youth later in His life. In 1868, "Once in Royal David's City" appeared in another hymnal with the melody "Irby." This is the version we love and sing today.

The carol starts with biblical lyrics. Royal David's city is Bethlehem,[18] which, at the time of Jesus' birth, boasted between 1500 and 2000 residents. It was an agriculturally-driven small town south of Jerusalem. Bethlehem's primary exports at the time were barley, wheat, and wool. It makes sense that there would be a "lowly cattle shed" with a manger where a desperate mother could lay her newborn boy. Stanza two begins by declaring Jesus to be God[19] and Lord of all.[20] Once the song is clear that Jesus is God, it returns to the theme of humility by explaining that His shelter was a stable and His cradle was a stall. The last two lines of the second stanza describe Jesus living with the poor,

---

[16] The title of this book is a play on the name of the "Lessons and Carols" service.
[17] Cecil Alexander penned over 400 hymns, including "There is a Green Hill Far Away," and "All Things Bright and Beautiful."
[18] Luke 2:4, "And Joseph also went up from Galilee, from the town of Nazareth to Judea, to the city of David, which is called Bethlehem, because he was of the house and lineage of David."
[19] John 1:1, "In the beginning was the Word, and the Word was with God, and the Word was God."
[20] Romans 10:9, "If you confess with your mouth that Jesus is Lord and believe in your heart that God raised Him from the dead, you will be saved."

mean, and lowly. During His life on earth, Jesus associated with the outcasts of society: sinners, tax collectors,[21] and Samaritans.[22]

The carol's third stanza presents some issues. We know that Jesus honored and obeyed His parents, but we don't know that Jesus' entire childhood was wondrous. The last two lines of the stanza deviate from Scripture and create theological issues. Alexander switched from focusing on the life of young Jesus to Victorian expectations of children: "Christian children all must be. Mild, obedient, good as He." Victorian England expected their children to be seen and not heard. Children were to be mild and obedient. But to say that children have to be as good as Jesus pushes the idea too far. In comparing children to Jesus, the author promotes salvation through works rather than grace. No child, no matter how sweet and precious, could ever compare to Jesus.

While stanzas one through three focus on the last time man saw Jesus, stanzas four and five shift the focus to the next time we will see Him. Stanza four speaks of the "Child so dear and gentle" being "our Lord in heaven above." The stanza reminds us that Jesus was Emmanuel – God with us. This baby boy was fully God and fully man. He is our Lord. Stanza five speaks of us seeing Him in heaven at God's right hand. This line is also straight out of the Apostles' Creed. Cecil Alexander had succeeded in her goal of teaching the children about Jesus being born of the virgin Mary and sitting at the right hand of God the Father almighty. Perhaps the carol is not only for children but for all of us; we all need to be reminded of who Jesus is and to try to be more like Him.

---

[21] Matthew 9:11, "And when the Pharisees saw this, they said to His disciples, "Why does your teacher eat with tax collectors and sinners?"
[22] John 4:1-45.

Silent Night, Holy Night

1. Si - lent night, Ho - ly night! All is calm, all is bright,
2. Si - lent night, Ho - ly night! Shep - herds quake at the sight!
3. Si - lent night, Ho - ly night! Son of God, love's pure light;
4. Si - lent night, Ho - ly night! Won - drous star, lend thy light;

'round yon vir - gin mo - ther and child; ho - ly in - fant, so ten - der and mild,
glo - ries stream from heav - en a - far, heav'n - ly hosts sing al - le - lu - jah;
ra - diant beams from Thy ho - ly face, With the dawn of re - deem - ing grace,
with the an - gels let us sing, "Al - le - lu - ia to our King;

sleep in hea - ven - ly peace, sleep in hea - ven - ly peace.
Christ, the Sa - vior, is born! Christ, the Sa - vior, is born!
Je - sus, Lord at Thy birth, Je - sus, Lord at Thy birth.
Christ the Sav - ior is born! Christ, the Sav - ior is born.

Lyrics: Joseph Mohr, 1816
Music: Franz Gruber, 1818
Arr. Timothy Mulder, 2025

23

Silent Night, Holy Night

———⋆⋆⋆———

LUKE 2:16

And they went with haste and found Mary and Joseph,
and the baby lying in a manger.

"SILENT NIGHT, HOLY NIGHT" IS the most recorded song in history. There are over 137,000 recorded versions of the beloved carol. Artists who have recorded the song include Alan Jackson, Mariah Carey, Frank Sinatra, Stevie Nicks, the Carpenters, Elvis Presley, and Bon Jovi. It has been sung in over 140 languages and remains one of the most popular carols of our time. But the song would never have been written if it hadn't been for a broken church organ.

In 1816, a young priest named Joseph Mohr penned the lyrics while walking to church with his grandfather one evening. He held onto them because he didn't know what to do with them. Two years later, Mohr was assigned to serve in the tiny Austrian village of Oberndorf. On Christmas Eve, Mohr prepared the church for the traditional midnight mass. He tried to play the organ, but it was broken. After several hours of tinkering with the organ, he visited the church organist, Franz Gruber,[23] to come up with a solution. Mohr provided the lyrics he had written years earlier and asked Gruber to develop a melody and harmony to accompany the guitar. After a few hours, Gruber appeared at the church and taught the music to the small church choir. It was sung at the midnight mass with guitar accompaniment.

Mohr began telling people about the carol and provided free copies to anyone who wanted them. A month later, Karl Mauracher, the traveling organ repairman, was given a copy, which he readily shared with other churches on his route. In 1854, King Frederick William IV, the King of Prussia, heard the carol and stipulated that "Silent Night, Holy Night" should be the first piece in the country's official Christmas concerts. Later on, troops sang the carol during the Civil War and World War I during Christmas truces. In these truces, armies would stop fighting and join in fellowship and song. They were a brief moment of reprieve in otherwise horrible wars. Today, the carol is frequently sung acapella during Christmas Eve candlelight services.

"Silent Night, Holy Night" is not a song about the night of Jesus' birth but rather the nights after that. Scripture tells us that the first night of Jesus' life on earth was anything but silent. Luke 2 reports that multitudes of angels praised God and that a group of shepherds paid Jesus a visit as well.

"Silent Night, Holy Night" is a lullaby sung to the baby Jesus. The first stanza speaks of the Virgin Mary being with Christ at His birth. The song states that as an infant, Jesus was tender and mild. In Matthew 11:29,[24] Jesus tells us that He is "gentle and lowly in heart." Jesus was not gentle and lowly or tender and mild during His infancy only. He was that way throughout His life, and, even now, as He intercedes for us in heaven, He is still tender and mild. Calling Jesus tender or gentle emphasizes His steadfast love for His people. Since Jesus is lowly and mild, He is humble and accessible. Since Jesus is all those things, we know that we can approach Him in prayer at any time and He will answer

---

[23] Franz Gruber is not to be confused with the fictional Hans Gruber, the villain from the Christmas film *Die Hard*.

[24] Matthew 11:29, "Take my yoke upon you, and learn from me, for I am gentle and lowly in heart, and you will find rest for your souls."

us.[25] The carol's first stanza concludes in lullaby form, telling the tender and mild newborn to sleep in heavenly peace.

The carol's second stanza speaks of the not-so-silent occurrences at Jesus' birth. According to the verse, an army of angels sang "Alleluia." Scripture does not tell us that the angels specifically sang "alleluia." Alleluia is a Hebrew word that means "Praise God."[26] And that is what the angels were doing: praising God! They were pronouncing that Christ, the Savior, had been born! And the angels were not quiet about it. That night was most certainly not "silent."

The third stanza refers to Jesus as the Son of God and love's pure light. John 3:16[27] tells us that Jesus was the Son of God. But what about "love's pure light?" Jesus, in John 8:12,[28] called Himself the light of the world. The most important line in the carol's third stanza is that with Jesus' birth came the dawn of redeeming grace. God, through the birth of His Son, ushered in the means of redeeming grace. Jesus Christ came to earth to live and die for those who believe. Our salvation began with the birth of Mary's precious baby boy.

---

[25] He always answers prayer: the answer will either be "yes," "no," or "not yet."

[26] Alleluia is a Hebrew compound word. The root word *hallel* means "praise," and the suffix *yah* means "Yahweh" or "Lord."

[27] John 3:16, "For God so loved the world, that He gave His only Son, that whoever believes in Him should not perish but have eternal life."

[28] John 8:12, "Again Jesus spoke to them, saying, 'I am the light of the world. Whoever follows me will not walk in darkness but will have the light of life.'"

The First Noel

1. The first No - el, the an - gel did say, was to cer - tain poor
2. They look - ed up and saw a star shin - ing in the
3. And by the light of that same star three wise men
4. This star drew nigh to the north - west, o'er Beth - le -
5. Then en - tered in those wise men three, full re - ver - ent -
6. Then let us all with one ac - cord sing prai - ses

shep - herds in fields as they lay; in fields where they lay keep - ing their
east, be - yond them far, and to the earth it gave great
came from coun - try far, to seek for king was their in -
hem it took its rest, and there it did both stop and
ly up - on their knee, and of - fered there in His pre -
to our hea - ven - ly Lord, who hath made heaven and earth of

sheep, on a cold win - ter's night that was ver so deep. No - el, No - el, No -
light, and so it con - ti - nued day and night.
tent, and fol - low the star wher - e - ver it went.
stay, right o - ver the place where Je - sus lay.
sence their gold, and myrrh, and fran - kin - cense.
naught, and with His blood our life hath bought.

el, No - el, born is the King of Is - ra - el.

Edited by William Sandys
Arranged by Davies Gilbert
Arr. Timothy Mulder, 2025

24

The First Noel

LUKE 2:11

For unto you is born this day in the city of David a Savior,
who is Christ the Lord.

"THE FIRST NOEL"[29] REFERS TO the angels' proclamation of the birth of Jesus Christ to the shepherds. There is some disagreement about the history of the word "Noel." Britons claim that its first use was by Chaucer in *The Canterbury Tales*. It was a joyous shout made on Christmas Day. However, French

---

[29] Noel, or Noël, or Nowell, has several different meanings. The general meaning is an exclamation made at Christmastime.

etymologists claim the word is theirs because it is rooted in the Latin word *natalis*, which means "birthday."

The carol dates back to the late fifteenth century when Bibles were not widely circulated, and most people could not read. The carol's author had heard the Christmas story many times but was a little fuzzy on the details. The carol's first two stanzas provide the story of the angels and the shepherds. The first line tells us that the angels proclaimed the first Noel to shepherds sleeping in the fields where they kept their sheep, which concurs with Luke 2:8-10.[30] However, the final line of the stanza states that it was wintertime. Most scholars believe that Jesus was born in the fall.

Stanza two claims that the shepherds followed the star, which shone in the east from a distance away. There are two biblical discrepancies with this verse. There is no mention in Luke 2 of the shepherds following the star. The star may have been there, and they may have followed it, but Scripture does not explicitly tell us that the shepherds followed the star. It does say, in Matthew 2:1-2,[31] that the wise men from the east followed the star. In this, the carol's third stanza agrees with Matthew 2:1-2. Geographically, however, the wise men would have seen the star to the west of their location, so the phrase "shining in the east" should more accurately read "shining in the west." The star gave off great light for the wise men to follow it. According to Matthew 2:2, they sought the king by following the star.

The carol's fourth stanza conflicts with the second verse; for now, the star is in the northwest rather than the east. Regardless of whether it was in the east or northwest, we know that the wise men followed it and, instead of traveling directly to Bethlehem, stopped in Jerusalem to inquire of Herod where the newborn king was located.[32] It was only after Herod's chief priests and scribes explained where the child was to be born that they headed on their way. The

---

[30] Luke 2:8-10, "And in the same region there were shepherds out in the field, keeping watch over their flock by night. [9] And an angel of the Lord appeared to them, and the glory of the Lord shone around them, and they were filled with great fear. [10] And the angel said to them, 'Fear not, for behold, I bring you good news of great joy that will be for all the people.'"

[31] Matthew 2:1-2, "Now after Jesus was born in Bethlehem of Judea in the days of Herod the king, behold, wise men from the east came to Jerusalem, [2] saying, "Where is He who has been born king of the Jews? For we saw His star when it rose and have come to worship Him."

[32] See also Matthew 2:2.

star, according to Matthew 2:9[33] led the wise men to Bethlehem and stopped over the place where the child was.

Stanza five describes the three wise men visiting the newborn Jesus. The Bible doesn't say how many wise men visited Jesus. Tradition numbers the wise men at three because they presented three gifts to Jesus. Matthew 2:11[34] tells us that they fell down and worshiped Him. In the time of Christ, "bending the knee" was the same as bowing to someone to show honor and respect.

The carol's last stanza turns from the story of the wise men to a charge to the listener. It commands us to sing praises to our heavenly Lord together, for He has made heaven and earth from nothing, but even more than that, with His blood, has paid for our sinful lives.

While "The First Noel" has its share of scriptural inaccuracies, its fervor and excitement regarding the newborn King of Israel more than make up for it. One cannot sing the carol without celebrating the birth of Jesus Christ, which is why we celebrate Christmas.

---

[33] Matthew 2:9, "After listening to the king, they went on their way. And behold, the star that they had seen when it rose went before them until it came to rest over the place where the child was."

[34] Matthew 2:11, "And going into the house, they saw the child with Mary, His mother, and they fell down and worshiped Him. Then, opening their treasures, they offered Him gifts, gold and frankincense and myrrh."

We Three Kings

1.We three kings of O - ri - ent are, Bear - ing gifts we trav - erse a - far Field and
2.Born a King in Beth - le - hem's plain, Gold I bring to crown Him a - gain, King for -
3.Frank in - cense to of - fer have I, In - cense owns a De - i - ty nigh; Prayer and
4.Myrrh is mine; it's bit - ter per - fume Breathes a life of gath - er - ing gloom; Sor - rowing
5.Glo - rious now be - hold Him a - rise, King and God and Sac - ri - fice; Al - le -

foun - tain, moor and moun - tain, Fol - low - ing yon - der star.
ev - er, ceas - ing nev - er O - ver us all to reign.
prais - ing, all men rais - ing, Wor - ship Him, God on high.   O___ star of won - der, star of night,
sigh - ing, bleed - ing dy - ing, Sealed in the stone-cold tomb.
lu - ia, Al - le - lu - ia! Peals through the earth and skies.

Star with roy - al beau - ty bright. West - ward lead - ing, still pro - ceed - ing, Guide us to thy per - fect Light.

John Henry Hopkins, 1863
Arr. Timothy Mulder, 2025

25

We Three Kings

MATTHEW 2:2

Where is He who has been born King of the Jews?
For we saw His star when it rose and have come to worship Him.

"WE THREE KINGS" PRESENTS THE story of the magi who followed the star to
Jesus in Bethlehem. They presented Jesus with gifts of gold, frankincense, and
myrrh.[35] The song's title speaks of three[36] "kings," but Scripture does not

---

[35] Matthew 2:11, "And going into the house, they saw the child with Mary His mother, and they
fell down and worshiped Him. Then, opening their treasures, they offered Him gifts, gold and
frankincense and myrrh."
[36] As discussed in "The First Noel," because there were three gifts, the general belief is that there
were three magi. The Bible doesn't tell us how many there were.

specify that they were kings. The Greek word used in Matthew 2 is *magos*, from which we get the English word "magic." Typically, magi were Mede and Persian priests who practiced astrology. This makes sense because they saw the Bethlehem star and followed it to the newborn King of the Jews, Jesus Christ. The "king" confusion may also stem from the princely gifts given by the magi as gold, frankincense, and myrrh were so costly as to be only afforded by royalty.

The author and composer of the carol was John Henry Hopkins, one of the top Episcopal church musicians in New England during the nineteenth century. Hopkins wrote the carol after reading the story of the magi in Matthew 2:1-12. In 1863, he published it in his collection of music entitled *Carols, Hymns, and Songs*. Because the carol is about the three magi, "We Three Kings" is typically sung during Epiphany.[37]

A trio of magi usually sings the carol's first verse together. It speaks of their arduous journey, traveling through fields, fountains, moors, and mountains to follow the star of Bethlehem. The carol says that the three kings were from the Orient, but the Bible describes the magi as being from the East, which could have been anywhere in the Asian continent. The chorus makes it seem like the star is being prayed to and praised. However, the last line of the chorus, "Guide us to thy perfect Light," shows that the purpose of the star is to lead the magi to the light of the world, Jesus Christ.

Jesus, while on earth, was our prophet, priest, and king. And each of the gifts of the magi symbolized one of those three roles. Matthew 2:11[38] tells us that the magi brought Jesus gifts of gold, frankincense, and myrrh. Gold was a gift for a king, frankincense was used in temple worship, and myrrh was used as an embalming agent. In stanzas 2, 3, and 4, the carol talks about the symbolic nature of those gifts. The gifts the magi brought to Jesus were part of God's provision for Mary, Joseph, and Jesus. The gold would have been used to support the family during their time in Egypt.[39]

---

[37] Epiphany is a Christian holiday celebrated on January 6. It celebrates the revelation of Jesus to the Gentile world, as initially shown in the Magi's visit.

[38] Matthew 2:11, "And going into the house, they saw the child with Mary, His mother, and they fell down and worshiped Him. Then, opening their treasures, they offered Him gifts, gold and frankincense and myrrh."

[39] Matthew 2:13-15, "Now when they had departed, behold, an angel of the Lord appeared to Joseph in a dream and said, "Rise, take the child and His mother, and flee to Egypt, and remain there until I tell you, for Herod is about to search for the child, to destroy Him." [14] And he rose and took the child and His mother by night and departed to Egypt [15] and remained there until the

Stanzas 2-4 are traditionally sung as solos by each magi. Stanza 2 has the magi bringing Jesus the gift of gold. Gold, in biblical times, was typically associated with kings. In the third line of the second verse, the magi declare that Christ will be King forever, never ceasing to reign over all. The magi, according to Matthew 2:2,[40] referred to Jesus as the King of the Jews. The magi recognized Jesus as a king, acknowledging His divine authority and destiny. The gold symbolizes Jesus' role as King of Kings.

The carol's third stanza speaks about the gift of frankincense. The gift of frankincense symbolized Jesus' priestly role, as it was typically used in the temple as incense during worship. In bringing the newborn Jesus frankincense, the magi acknowledged Jesus as God and the ultimate High Priest. Frankincense symbolizes Jesus' role as the great High Priest.

Stanza 4 brings up the final gift of myrrh. Myrrh was a precious perfume often used during the embalming stage of preparing a body for burial. Therefore, the gift of myrrh symbolized His sacrificial death. The rest of the fourth stanza speaks of the death and burial of Jesus. A prophet was an individual who represented God and brought His word to mankind. Jesus was all at the same time: a prophet,[41] God, and the Word.[42] The gift of myrrh symbolized the death that He would undergo to redeem His people.

The carol's final stanza tells us to look up at the resurrected Jesus, who has risen from the grave and taken His rightful place as King. In the final days, at the name of Jesus, every knee should bow and confess that Jesus Christ is Lord.[43] The carol concludes with singing alleluia to Jesus Christ our Lord. Those alleluias are heard throughout the world and the skies. Let us all sing to Him in boundless joy.

---

death of Herod. This was to fulfill what the Lord had spoken by the prophet, "Out of Egypt I called my son."

[40] Matthew 2:2, "Where is He who has been born King of the Jews? For we saw His star when it rose and have come to worship Him."

[41] Acts 3:22, "Moses said, 'The Lord God will raise up for you a prophet like me from your brothers. You shall listen to Him in whatever He tells you."

[42] John 1:1-3 tells us that Jesus was both God and the Word. "In the beginning was the Word, and the Word was with God, and the Word was God. 2 He was in the beginning with God. 3 All things were made through Him, and without Him was not anything made that was made."

[43] Philippians 2:10-11, "So that at the name of Jesus every knee should bow, in heaven and on earth and under the earth, 11 and every tongue confess that Jesus Christ is Lord, to the glory of God the Father."

What Child is This? (Greensleeves)

1.What Child is this, who laid to rest on Ma – ry's lap is sleep – ing? Whom
2.Why lies He in such mean es – tate, where ox and ass are feed – ing? Good
3.So bring Him in – cense, gold, and myrrh, come peas – ant, king, to own Him. The

an – gels greet with an – thems sweet,___ While shep – herds watch___ are keep – ing?
Chris – tian fear; for sin – ners here the sil – ent Word is plead – ing.
King of kings, sal – va – tion brings, Let lov – ing hearts en – throne Him.

This, this is Christ the King; Whom shep – herds guard___ and an – gels sing:
Nails, spear shall pierce Him through; the cross be born for me and you:
Raise, raise the song on high, The vir – gin sings her lull – a – by:

Haste, haste___ to bring Him laud,___ the Babe, the Son of Ma – ry.
Hail, hail, the Word made flesh, the Babe, the Son of Ma – ry.
Joy, joy for Christ is born, the Babe, the Son of Ma – ry.

William Chatterton Dix, 1865
Arr. Timothy Mulder, 2025

26

What Child is This? (Greensleeves)

———⟡———

LUKE 2:16

And they went with haste and found Mary and Joseph,
and the baby lying in a manger.

THE MELODY OF "WHAT CHILD IS THIS?" (Greensleeves) has existed in written form since 1580, when it was registered to Richard Jones. However, Greensleeves was a popular drinking song for hundreds of years before that. Due to its age, Greensleeves has had over twenty different lyrics associated with it. Even King Henry VIII is rumored to have written lyrics to Greensleeves while courting Anne Boleyn. The melody will be forever associated with King Henry since Shakespeare used it in his play *The Merry Wives of Windsor*. By the nineteenth century, Greensleeves had become so popular in Britain that it rivaled "God Save the Queen."

The lyrics to "What Child is This?" were written in 1865 by Scottish marine insurance agent William Chatterton Dix, who wrote poetry on the side. Dix also penned "As With Gladness Men of Old" and "Alleluia! Sing to Jesus!" Many of Dix's hymns were written during a period of crippling depression. It seems that the hymns served as a way to lift his spirits. When Dix wrote the lyrics for "What Child Is This?", Christmas was not the commercial celebration it is today. Conservative Christian churches forbade gift-giving, decorating, or even acknowledging Christmas. In this context, it was unusual for Dix to write about Christ's birth, since most authors of the period ignored Christmas altogether. Dix's poem was known as "The Manger Throne," and became popular in the U.S. as the Civil War ended. It was frequently used in church services in both America and England. However, it wasn't until an unnamed Englishman put Dix's poem to the tune of Greensleeves that it became immensely popular. Since he lived until 1898, Dix witnessed his poem become the popular Christmas carol, "What Child is This?"

The carol's lyrics provide a unique view of the birth of Christ. While the baby Jesus is the song's focal point, the author's perspective is that of a confused observer. Employing this perspective, Dix wove together the story of the child's birth, life, death, and resurrection. Each stanza answers with a triumphant declaration of the infant's divine nature.

All three stanzas contain content from Philippians 2:6-11.[44] The carol's first stanza is based on Philippians 2:7, which tells us that Jesus was born like other men, even though He was fully God. Describing the newborn baby as asleep on His mother's lap, the stanza shows us that He was born just like any other human being. Philippians 2:8 and the carol's second stanza speak to the humiliation of Christ. According to the carol, Jesus was born into a "mean estate," meaning His surroundings were noisy and dirty. After all, oxen and asses were feeding, and Jesus was lying in one of the troughs from which they ate. But it wasn't only the surroundings of Jesus' birth that were mean. While

---

[44] Philippians 2:6-11 – "Who, though He was in the form of God, did not count equality with God a thing to be grasped, [7] but emptied Himself, by taking the form of a servant, being born in the likeness of men. [8] And being found in human form, He humbled Himself by becoming obedient to the point of death, even death on a cross. [9] Therefore God has highly exalted Him and bestowed on Him the name that is above every name, [10] so that at the name of Jesus every knee should bow, in heaven and on earth and under the earth, [11] and every tongue confess that Jesus Christ is Lord, to the glory of God the Father."

much of His life was difficult, the last week of His life was an especially "mean estate." The second stanza also speaks of the mean estate of Jesus' death. Jesus, after being scourged with a cat of nine tails, had to carry His 250 lb. cross on His bloody back. In the process of crucifying Him, nails pierced His hands. A spear pierced His side. His flesh was torn and bloody. He had been utterly humiliated by those He died to save. This was "the Word made flesh."

The carol's third stanza discusses the exaltation of Jesus, which can be found in Philippians 2:9-11. As discussed in "We Three Kings," the magi brought Jesus gold, frankincense, and myrrh. Dix calls the magi "peasant kings," who brought Him the three gifts. The third line in the carol's third stanza presents the gospel: "The King of kings salvation brings." Jesus' birth began the earthly process of saving His chosen people. Salvation will come only through this newborn King of kings.[45] Outside of Him, there is no other way to be saved. Acts 4:12 tells us, "And there is salvation in no one else, for there is no other name under heaven given among men by which we must be saved."[46] The second part of the carol's third verse, like many other carols, ends in outright praise: "Raise, raise the song on high" and "Joy, joy for Christ is born, the Babe, the Son of Mary. Christmas is a time of celebration, and "What Child Is This?" allows us to indeed raise a song on high to laud the King of kings.

---

[45] Revelation 17:14, "They will make war on the Lamb, and the Lamb will conquer them, for He is Lord of lords and *King of kings*, and those with Him are called and chosen and faithful." (Italics added.)

[46] In John 14:6, Jesus tells us that He is the only way in which we are saved: "Jesus said to him, 'I am the way, and the truth, and the life. No one comes to the Father except through me."

While Shepherds Watched Their Flocks by Night

Nahum Tate, 1562
George Frideric Handel
Arr. Timothy Mulder, 2025

27

While Shepherds Watched Their Flocks by Night

───────⚜───────

LUKE 2:8

And in the same region there were shepherds out in the field,
keeping watch over their flock by night.

WHEN "WHILE SHEPHERDS WATCHED THEIR Flocks by Night" was written, the psalms were the only thing sung in churches. "Exclusive psalmody"[47] was the usual practice then. One of the primary arrangers of the Psalms was a musician named Nahum Tate. Tate would paraphrase a psalm and turn it into something that could be sung to a rhythm. Tate and Nicholas Brady, a canon at Cork Cathedral in Ireland, published *A New Version of the Psalms of David* in

───────────────

[47] Exclusive psalmody is still practiced in some churches, where singing only Psalms is practiced.

1696. This hymnal replaced the outdated *The Whole Booke of Psalms*, which had been published in 1562. Many congregants hated the new-fangled versions of the Psalms and preferred the ones they had sung for years.

Tate authored "While Shepherds Watched Their Flocks by Night," which was a metrical version of Luke 2:8-14[48] (as found in the King James Bible) and included it in a supplement to the 1696 hymnal. The supplement indicated that the lyrics could be sung to any song of common meter. One of the most popular tunes was "Winchester,"[49] written by Thomas Ravenscroft. This is the tune most commonly used in England and can be heard in the annual broadcast of the King's College Service of Nine Lessons and Carols. Americans, however, prefer to use the tune "Christmas" by George Frideric Handel.

This is one of those carols that ought to be sung more often. It is completely scriptural. So when we sing it, we immerse ourselves in God's Word. Of all the carols in this book, "While Shepherds Watched Their Flocks" is the closest to Scripture. The carol's first stanza tells us that shepherds were watching their flocks by night, and the angel of the Lord came down and glory shone all around. Luke 2:8-9 (KJV) says, "And there were in the same country shepherds abiding in the field, *keeping watch over their flock by night.* And, lo, the *angel of the Lord came* upon them, and *the glory of the Lord shone round* about them: and they were sore afraid." (Italics added.) The only thing in the carol's first stanza that is not scriptural is that the shepherds were all seated on the ground. The carol's second stanza is just as solid. The angels said, "Fear not!" and brought glad tidings of great joy to all mankind. Luke 2:10 (KJV) says, "And *the angel said unto them, Fear not:* for, behold, I bring you good tidings of great joy, which shall be to all people."

Continuing with its biblical paraphrasing, the carol's third stanza speaks of a Savior, Christ the Lord, who is born to you this day in David's town and of David's line. Luke 2:11 (KJV) says, "For *unto you is born this day in the city of David a Savior, which is Christ the Lord.*" (Italics added.) The stanza follows the Bible almost word for word. Stanza three ends with the line, "and this shall

---

[48] Luke 2:8-14, (KJV) "And there were in the same country shepherds abiding in the field, keeping watch over their flock by night. [9] And, lo, the angel of the Lord came upon them, and the glory of the Lord shone round about them: and they were sore afraid. [10] And the angel said unto them, Fear not: for, behold, I bring you good tidings of great joy, which shall be to all people. [11] For unto you is born this day in the city of David a Savior, which is Christ the Lord. [12] And this shall be a sign unto you; Ye shall find the babe wrapped in swaddling clothes, lying in a manger. [13] And suddenly there was with the angel a multitude of the heavenly host praising God, and saying, [14] 'Glory to God in the highest, and on earth peace, good will toward men.'"

[49] Winchester is now known as Old Winchester, and is the version included in this book.

be a sign," which is the first part of Luke 2:12. The rest of Luke 2:12 (KJV) says that the shepherds "*shall find the babe wrapped in swaddling clothes, lying in a manger.*" (Italics added.) The carol's fourth stanza tells us that the angel told the shepherds that they would find the heavenly babe wrapped in swaddling cloths and laid in a manger.

The fifth stanza of the carol addresses the multitude of angels praising God. Luke 2:13 (KJV) says, "And suddenly *there was with the angel a multitude of the heavenly host praising God.*" (Italics added.) The carol's fifth stanza says that the seraph spoke, and when he had finished, there was a throng of angels praising God." Luke 2:13 says there was a "multitude of the heavenly host." What is that? Revelation 5:11[50] tells us that there were myriads of myriads and thousands of thousands of angels. A heavenly host or a host of angels is an army of angels. And they are numbered in the millions. Have you ever heard a group of several hundred people singing joyfully? It is loud. Can you imagine millions of angels praising God together? That would be both awesome and deafening.

The carol's final stanza is based on Luke 2:14 (KJV), which has the angels proclaiming, "*Glory to God in the highest, and on earth peace, good will toward men.*"[51] (Italics added.) The carol's sixth stanza follows the Bible exactly, saying, "All glory be to God on high, and to the earth peace and good will from heaven to men."

"While Shepherds Watched Their Flocks By Night" is a fantastic Christmas carol that should be sung more often, if nothing else, for its scriptural basis.

---

[50] Revelation 5:11, "Then I looked, and I heard around the throne and the living creatures and the elders the voice of many angels, numbering myriads of myriads and thousands of thousands."

[51] Interestingly, Luke 2:14 (KJV) is different that Luke 2:14 (ESV). Luke 2:14 in the ESV reads, "Glory to God in the highest, and on earth peace among those with whom he is pleased!" The KJV is missing the phrase "with whom He is pleased." This is because the KJV was based on the manuscripts available in 1611. The ESV is based on much older manuscripts of Scripture. Therefore, the ESV is closer to the original text.

Within a Crib My Savior Lay

1.With - in____ a crib my Sav - ior lay, a wood - en man - ger filled__ with hay, come down for love__ on Christ - mas Day: all glo - ry be__ to Je - sus!

2.Up - on____ a cross my Sav - ior died, to ran - som sin - ners, cru - ci - fied, His lov - ing arms__ still o - pen wide: all glo - ry be__ to Je - sus!

3.A vic - tor's crown my Sav - ior won, His work of love and mer - cy done, the Fa - ther's high - as - cend - ed Son: all glo - ry be__ to Je - sus!

Timothy Dudley-Smith, 1968
Arr. Timothy Mulder, 2025

28

Within a Crib My Savior Lay

———◦══════◦⟨◆⟩◦══════◦———

1 JOHN 4:10

*In this is love, not that we have loved God but that He loved us
and sent His Son to be the propitiation for our sins.*

THE NEWEST CHRISTMAS CAROL IN our book is also the last one. The lyrics for
"Within a Crib My Savior Lay" were written in 1968 by Timothy Dudley-
Smith, a bishop of the Church of England, who wrote approximately 400
hymns. Dudley-Smith was part of the British "hymn explosion" after World
War II. In the early 1960s, Dudley-Smith published two hymn books: one for
everyday church use and the other specifically for youth. He is most famous for
his hymn, "Tell Out, My Soul."

The music for the carol was written by Norman Warren, an ordained priest in the Church of England and prolific hymn writer. Warren has published many different songbooks and collections of music, and his best-selling evangelistic booklet, *Journey into Life*, has worldwide sales of 30 million. Warren put Dudley-Smith's lyrics to his tune, "Lord of Love," in 1982.

"Within a Crib My Savior Lay" is unique because it is not based on a Christmas text, such as Matthew 1 or Luke 2. Instead, it is based on 1 John 4:10. This verse tells us that God loved us and sent His Son to propitiate[52] our sins. Jesus Christ was born to appease God's wrath towards mankind's sin and to reconcile man to God. Jesus offered Himself as a sacrifice to make us right with God. Jesus' sacrifice was comprised of three steps, each of which is covered in one of the carol's stanzas.

There are two primary themes in the carol's lyrics. The first theme is that Jesus is "my Savior." Each stanza calls Jesus "my Savior," making a personal statement about what Jesus has done. Jesus, "my Savior," was found in the manger. Jesus "my Savior," was crucified for His chosen people. Jesus, "my Savior," rose from the dead and ascended into heaven. John 3:16 clearly explains Jesus' role: "For God so loved the world, that He gave His only Son, that whoever believes in Him should not perish but have eternal life." Jesus' sole purpose in coming to earth and humiliating Himself was to be our Savior.[53] For Jesus to save us, we must have a personal faith in Him. A completely academic faith will avail us nothing. It must be a deep, personal faith.

The second theme in the carol is the final line of each verse: "All glory be to Jesus!" Because Jesus came to earth to save us, we are to offer Him thanks and praise for His amazing act of love. In all we do, we should offer all glory to Jesus.

The carol's first stanza speaks of Jesus' incarnation. Jesus was born of flesh and blood just like you and I were. While fully God, He is also fully human. And as a human, He was a child with needs typical of a child. He lay in a crib, which, at His birth, was a wooden manger that was filled with hay. He appeared to be a normal baby boy like any other. He got tired and needed naps. He cried

---

[52] Propitiate means appeasing the wrath of an offended person and being reconciled to him.

[53] Philippians 2:5-8, "Have this mind among yourselves, which is yours in Christ Jesus, 6 who, though He was in the form of God, did not count equality with God a thing to be grasped, 7 but emptied Himself, by taking the form of a servant, being born in the likeness of men. 8 And being found in human form, He humbled Himself by becoming obedient to the point of death, even death on a cross."

when He got hungry. He had dirty diapers. He was fully human and fully God. And for His coming down to earth, we must offer Him all glory.

The next stanza speaks of Jesus' crucifixion. The first line says, "Upon a cross my Savior died." This is the first part of propitiation. Jesus, in dying on the cross, satisfied the wrath of God on behalf of His sinful people. In His death, Jesus ransomed sinners. Mark 10:45 says, "For even the Son of Man came not to be served but to serve, and to give His life as a ransom for many." This was the entire point of Jesus' life. He didn't come to be served, but to give up His life as a ransom for sinners. And He did this while we hated Him. Romans 5:18 says, "But God shows His love for us in that while we were still sinners, Christ died for us." We don't have to have our lives all together before we come to Jesus. He died while we were still sinners. His loving arms are open wide for us, regardless of where we are in our walk with Him. And for that, Jesus alone should receive all the glory!

The carol's final stanza moves from Jesus' crucifixion to His glorification. After Jesus was crucified, He died, was buried, and then on the third day, rose again from the dead. Forty days later, He ascended into Heaven where He sits victorious at the right hand of God the Father. When Jesus was resurrected from the dead, He was victorious over sin and death. As such, He offers eternal life to us. Jesus, in John 10:25-26, says, "I am the resurrection and the life. Whoever believes in me, though he die, yet shall he live, and everyone who lives and believes in me shall never die." This was His life's work – to show love and mercy to sinners and to win salvation for His chosen people. So, how are we to respond? We are to offer all glory to Him!

Though not based on the traditional verses of the nativity, this carol reminds us of the fact that without Jesus' death on the cross and resurrection from the dead, His birth would be but an interesting anecdote. The celebration of Christ's birth is the perfect time to proclaim the gospel and this beautifully concise carol makes that easy.

PLEASE REVIEW

★ ★ ★ ★ ★

You have reached the awkward part of the book where I ask you to leave me a review on Amazon, Google, or Goodreads. Believe me, I hate this as much as you do. However, I am swallowing my pride and asking anyway. Please! Whether you loved or hated it, you have made it this far, so please leave a review. Here's the thing: reviews play a big role in determining whether or not someone will read my book. Leaving a review will help me out a lot. If you liked this study, please recommend it to others. Oh, and thanks for reading my book. It means the world to me.

~~Sin in exultation!~~   Sing in exultation!

I can't stand typos. If you are like me, you can't either. Typos are like gremlins. No matter how many times a book has been edited, they magically appear. So, if you find an error, please don't hesitate to email me at timothyjmulder@gmail.com.

Thanks!

More by Timothy J. Mulder

Scan here to order:

Ruth: A Story of God's Redeeming Love

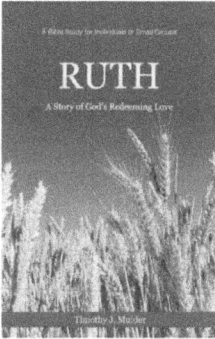

The Book of Ruth is one of the most famous short stories of all time. In just four chapters, the reader is exposed to faithlessness, death, unwavering integrity, and redemption. Ruth provides an intimate view into the back story of the lineage of King David. Set in the time of the Judges, when "everyone did what was right in their own eyes," the wholesomeness and honesty of Ruth are a welcome breath of fresh air. In this best-selling study, we cover such topics as God's loving-kindness, the foreshadowing of Christ, waiting on God's timing, the providence of God, and the redemption of Naomi. Join the author as he takes an in-depth, Reformed look into one of the greatest redemption stories of all time.

Jonah: God's Holy Runaway

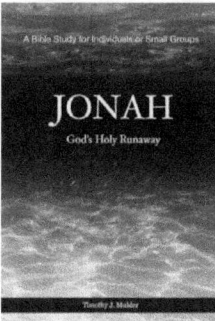

The Book of Jonah is far different than what we have been taught in Sunday School, acted out with a felt board whale, Jonah, and an evil Nineveh. It is not primarily about the fish. The Book of Jonah contains so much more: nationalism, hatred, unspeakable violence, and pagan omens. In it, the reader encounters a series of unexpected shocks. Jonah foolishly ran *from* God, while Gentile sailors ran *to* God. Jonah was thrown overboard and swallowed by a large fish. After Jonah delivered one of the worst calls to repentance, the entire city of Nineveh repented and turned toward God. This small book of 1368 words contains tales of storms and seas, winds blowing in the desert sands, a fish with a considerable gut, a fast-growing plant, Sheol, and penitent pagans. It challenges our preconceived notions about who the Gospel is for and hits at the heart of deeply held religious discrimination. Jonah is about second chances, bringing death to life, and how salvation belongs to the Lord.

The Despicable Dozen – Bad Guys of the Bible

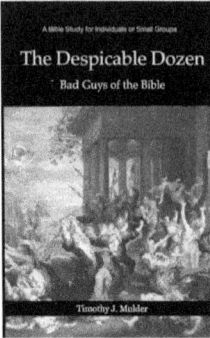

Browse any Christian bookseller, and you will see plenty of Bible studies on the heroes of the faith. What about the terrible, evil people in the Scriptures? God's inerrant Word includes these villains for a reason. Why are there no Bible studies about them? We know that God uses the "good guys" and the "bad guys" of the Bible to accomplish His perfect will. This study looks at the baddest of the bad: the despicable dozen.

The twelve villains in this study include those guilty of heinous sins, while others are included because of *whom* they sinned against. Our study will examine liars, adulterers, traitors, murderers, corrupt politicians, human traffickers, and despots guilty of murder and infanticide on an unfathomable scale. Upon finishing this study, you should better understand the sovereignty of God: His ability to use good and evil to accomplish His perfect, eternal plan.

What's Wrong With the Chosen?

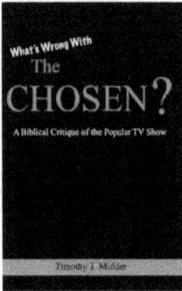

The Chosen is arguably the most well-received religious television series ever. It has received rave reviews, including a 9.8 out of 10 rating at IMDB. According to the show's producers, over 108 million people have watched since December 2022. It has been translated into over 50 languages and has multiple Bible studies based on its content. With such widespread support, what could be wrong with it? Is *The Chosen* biblically accurate? Does it matter? A poll of reformed pastors and teachers showed that 87% are concerned about unbiblical content and consider the show a threat to uninformed believers. *What's Wrong With The Chosen?* provides a biblical critique of the show. The author's four objections to *The Chosen* are discussed, followed by an in-depth analysis in which every scene in seasons 1-5 are evaluated for historical and Biblical accuracy.

The Armchair Theologian's Guide to the
Westminster Confession of Faith

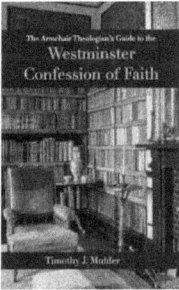

Do you ever feel as though you have read your Bible but wish you could better explain what you believe? Do you wonder how the Bible applies to our world today? Are you frustrated when confronted with viewpoints that are not Scriptural, but struggle to disprove them? The Westminster Confession of Faith is a topical arrangement of the Bible into doctrinal truths. It was written to organize the Bible into a unifying summary of what Christians believe and to combat heresy. The Westminster Confession of Faith is as relevant today as when it was written nearly 400 years ago. This book goes through the WCF in a user-friendly format, which includes the traditional and modern English versions of the WCF. It also highlights and counters unbiblical doctrine and creates talking points perfect for explaining Scripture to young believers or for cozy armchair discussions with friends.

Suffering in Silence: Ministering to Those With Mental Illness

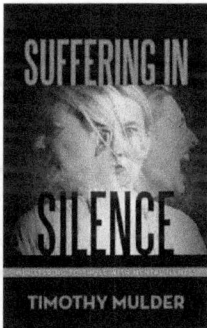

Mental illness affects millions of Americans. Often, those afflicted will develop substance abuse problems or will die from suicide. Surely, there must be something the church can do to help. The author considers questions such as: Why are those who suffer from mental illness so often misunderstood? What are common misconceptions about mental illness in the church? How are churches and other ministries well positioned to help people struggling with mental illness? How can you best minister to those with mental illness? Join the author as he explores how to better understand mental illness, so you may better minister to those who suffer from it.

www.ingramcontent.com/pod-product-compliance
Lightning Source LLC
LaVergne TN
LVHW021351080426
835508LV00020B/2228